OW TO BE A WINNER AT CHESS

Also by Fred Rein

CHESS MASTERY BY QUESTION AND ANSWER
THE NINE BAD MOVES OF CHESS
THE COMPLETE CHESSPLAYER
THE HUMAN SIDE OF CHESS

HOW TO BE A WINNER AT *Chess*

BY FRED REINFELD

With drawings by PETER ESTIN

FAWCETT COLUMBINE • NEW YORK

A Fawcett Columbine Book
Published by Ballantine Books

http://www.randomhouse.com

Library of Congress Catalog Card Number: 96-96631

ISBN: 0-449-91206-X

This edition published by arrangement with
Doubleday & Company, Inc.

Manufactured in the United States of America

First Fawcett Crest Edition: December 1970
First Ballantine Books Mass Market Edition: January 1985
First Ballantine Books Trade Edition: August 1996

10 9 8 7 6 5 4 3 2 1

FOR MY WIFE
who asked for a chess book that she could read

CONTENTS

INTRODUCTION

This book is the result of more than twenty years' thought about the problems of the average chessplayer and what he needs to learn to improve his game.

I have tried in every way I know to make this book an effective tool for becoming a much better chessplayer. The emphasis has been on those basic problems that turn up in every game. My hope has been to give the reader the goal, the purpose, the incentive which he may not previously have seen in the game of chess.

My aim has been to preserve the light touch. The technical approach and the grim, forbidding attitude have been ruled out. I have tried to present complicated subjects in the simplest language that has ever appeared in a chess book. The chess notation, the traditional stumbling block of most chess readers, has been made as painless as possible.

Players of any degree of strength can benefit by studying this book. Those already familiar with the rules of chess will find it useful to read the refresher material be-

ginning on page 175. Even complete beginners, who know nothing at all about chess, will be able to read this book profitably after first learning the basic rules which are explained on page 175 and succeeding pages.

I want to thank Harold Kuebler, my editor, for his invaluable aid in helping me show the reader "how to be a winner at chess."

FRED REINFELD

HOW TO BE A WINNER AT CHESS

CHAPTER 1

HOW TO END IT ALL

Checkmating

When I first learned to play chess as a youngster of twelve, I thought it was a wonderful game. I still do — after more than thirty years of playing, studying, talking, teaching, writing. What makes chess so fascinating and so tantalizing, I suppose, is that it's an unbeatable mixture of the complicated and the simple, the difficult and the easy.

Yes, it's a wonderful game, even though there are 169,-518,829,100,544,000,000,000,000,000 ways to play the first ten moves! Check the figures or take my word for it — either way we're on safe ground if we say there are zillions of possibilities in a game of chess.

Does that make chess a complicated game? Yes . . . and no. True, it's complicated in the number of possibilities involved. But — and most of us tend to forget this — chess has a very simple and clear-cut objective.

You win by checkmating your opponent's King — by attacking the King in such a way that no matter how he plays, his King will still remain under attack. This clear-cut objective makes chess an easy game.

Three Tests for Checkmate

There's an old saying among chess players:

"Always check, it might be mate!"

Usually made jokingly, this remark points up the most important feature of chess: *you win by checkmating your opponent's King*. Obvious as this sounds, all too many players forget about it in the heat of the battle. Others play aimlessly, at a loss for a guiding idea, content to play from move to move.

More than once I have come into a chess club and watched a game between two inexperienced players who had checkmated each other *without knowing it!* Such unawareness makes a farce out of the game. Let's be clear, then, at the very outset, just what we mean by "check" and "checkmate."

When you give check, you are attacking your opponent's King. When you give checkmate, you are attacking your opponent's King in such a way that the King cannot escape.

Every checkmate is a check; but not every check is a checkmate! To grasp the difference, you have to follow through every check to one of its three possible conclusions:

1. *the checking piece is captured* (Diagram 1).

White has just played his Queen to check Black's King by *Queen to King Rook 8* (Q–KR8 ch). Black disposes of the check by capturing White's Queen with his Bishop . . . *Bishop takes Queen* (. . . BxQ). With the disap-

Diagram 1 (*Black to play*)

BLACK

WHITE

pearance of the White Queen, Black's King is no longer in check. This was a check, but not a checkmate.

2. *a piece is interposed between the checking piece and the checked King* (Diagram 2).

Diagram 2 (*Black to play*)

BLACK

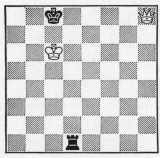

WHITE

In this position, too, White has just played his Queen

to check Black's King at King Rook. Black cannot capture the checking Queen. He has a different way of getting out of check: he interposes his Rook to shield his King from attack.

Black's move in Diagram 2, then, is . . . *Rook to King 1* (. . . R–K1). This cuts off the attack on his King, which is no longer in check. Again, this was a check, but not a checkmate.

3. *the checked King moves out of the line of attack* (Diagram 3).

Diagram 3 (*Black to play*)

BLACK

WHITE

Once more White has played *Queen to King Rook 8 check* (Q–KR8 ch). Black cannot capture the Queen, nor can he interpose a piece to ward off the attack. Luckily, his King can save himself, on the principle of "the gods help those who help themselves."

Let's see . . . Black's King can move, but where? To

play one square directly to the right — *King to Queen Bishop 1* (. . . K–QB1) — would be no help; the King would still be in check.

To play one square diagonally to the left — *King to Queen Rook 2* (. . . K–QR2) — would not do either, as Black cannot play his King to a square controlled by White's King.

Playing one square down the page — *King to Queen Knight 2* (. . . K–QN2) — is impossible for the same reason.

But Black does have a way out — one square diagonally to the right — . . . *King to Queen Bishop 2* (. . . K–QB2). This "flight square" is not commanded by White's King or Queen, and thus the Black King is out of check. Again, this was a check, but not a checkmate.

Checkmate

So far the checked King has had a way out each time. But if these defensive methods are not available, then we have a case of checkmate, as in Diagram 4. Some checkmates are planned far ahead; others come as a terrible surprise, as in the case of the heavily bearded player who lifts his beard at the critical moment — only to disclose a Rook that gives checkmate on the spot!

As you will see later on, whiskers are not the only way to hide a coming checkmate. When we say that a checkmate comes as a surprise, what we really mean is that the victim had his mind on other things and completely missed the danger that was threatening his King. Now let's look at our first diagram showing a foolproof checkmate:

Diagram 4 (*Final position*)

BLACK

WHITE

As in the previous diagrams, Black is in check. He cannot capture the checking Queen; he cannot interpose to cut off the line of attack; his King has no flight square to escape to.

Of the five "possible" squares to which the Black King might move, two — directly to the right or left — are still in the checking range of White's Queen. The other three squares — on Black's second rank — are all commanded by White's King. These conditions fill the requirements for checkmate!

More Checkmates

Here's another mate, in which the White King is the victim:

Diagram 5 (*Final position*)

BLACK

WHITE

(Remember, as you study Diagram 5, that Black Pawns move *toward the White side*, or down the page; also, that Pawns move straight ahead but capture diagonally.)

Black, you will note, is giving check with his Rook at Queen Bishop 6 (QB6). White cannot capture this Rook, which is guarded by the Black Pawn at Queen Knight 5 (QN5). Remember, you can never make a move which exposes your King to capture!

What other possibilities does White have in Diagram 5? He cannot capture the checking Rook. He cannot interpose to the check. Can he move his King out of danger?

The answer is still no. It is impossible for the King to move one square diagonally up to the left — . . . *King to*

Queen Bishop 4 (. . . K–QB4) — as that would expose
the King to capture by the Black Rook or the Black Queen
Pawn.

Likewise, to move one square diagonally to the right —
. . . *King to King 4* (K–K4) — would expose White's
King to capture by Black's Queen Pawn.

Two other possible moves remain. A move to the square
to the right — . . . *King to King 3* (K–K3) — is ruled out
because it still leaves the White King in check to Black's
Rook. It also exposes the White King to attack by Black's
Bishop.

Nor will a move one square backward do — . . . *King
to Queen 2* (K–Q2) — for that would still leave White's
King attacked by Black's long-range Bishop. Thus White's
King has no way out.

Then . . . this is checkmate? Yes, for White's King is
in check, and no matter what he does, he will still be in
check. Diagram 5 is a perfect example of checkmate.

So is Diagram 6, except that the checkmate hasn't happened yet. It's Black's move, and he is about to give checkmate on his very next move:

In Diagram 6 Black plays . . . *Knight to King Knight
6 check* (. . . N–KN6 ch). It may come as a shock to
you to be told this is a checkmate position!

True, White cannot capture the obstreperous Knight.
But the square to the immediate left of the King . . .
King to Knight 1 (K–N1) . . . seems available. Unfortu-

Diagram 6 (*Black to play*)

BLACK

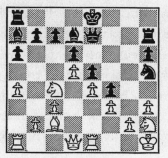

WHITE

nately it isn't! See that Black Bishop lurking all the way at the end of the diagonal at the upper left-hand corner of Diagram 6? That Black Bishop controls every square on the diagonal. Since White's King cannot walk into the Black Bishop's jurisdiction, *King to Knight 1* (K–N1) is ruled out. So White is checkmated.

Diagram 7 (*White to play*)

BLACK

WHITE

In Diagram 7 we have another position in which check-mate on the move is possible.

Diagram 7 is taken from a real game in which only a few moves have been played. And yet, believe it or not, White can force checkmate right off by playing *Bishop to Queen Knight 5 check* (B–QN5 ch).

This is checkmate, because the attacking Bishop cannot be captured; because Black has no interposing move to save his King; and finally, because his King cannot move out of check.

Thus, a move of the King one space diagonally: . . . *King to Queen 2* (. . . K–Q2) . . . still leaves the Black King exposed to attack from the checking Bishop.

Likewise . . . *King to King 2* (. . . K–K2) or . . . *King to Queen 1* (. . . K–Q1) is impossible. Either of those moves would expose the Black King to attack by the other White Bishop — the one that travels on black squares.

Again we have a case of checkmate — Black's King has no escape.

The basic idea in a game of chess, then, is to enforce checkmate on your opponent's King and to avoid getting checkmated yourself. Diagrams 4, 5, 6, and 7 show you how it's done.

Remember, you can avoid a checkmate if you can make any one of these three moves:

1. Capture the checking piece.

2. Interpose a piece between the checking piece and your King.

3. Move the checked King out of the line of attack.

CHAPTER 2

DON'T GIVE UP THE SHIP!

Resigning

As you've just seen, checkmate is the objective in every game of chess.

This doesn't mean, however, that every won game winds up with checkmate. Very often a player "resigns" — concedes his opponent's victory before checkmate actually takes place.

Now why in the world, you may wonder, should a player surrender before he is actually beaten? What kind of position does he have that makes him feel his "resignation" is in order?

A player resigns when he sees his position is hopeless.

Diagram 8 (page 31) is a good example. Black resigns because he cannot avoid checkmate on the very next move. Some players feel they "save face" by resigning instead of submitting to checkmate.

The other main reason for resigning is a crushing loss of material. In Diagram 9 (page 32) Black loses his Queen, by far the most powerful piece on the board. There is no hope for him now, and no fun in dragging out the game.

"A simple 'I resign' will do, general."

When to Resign

There are some quirks to resigning that you need to know about.

Some players are very stubborn and play on long after all hope is gone. Thus they waste their opponent's time and their own. Others are all too fainthearted and resign too readily. This is just as great a fault.

Of course there is a golden mean between these two extremes. It is pointless to resign too quickly. No general ever won a battle by surrendering, and no chess player ever won a game by resigning.

I once saw Reuben Fine, one of the world's greatest players, resign a very important match game because he thought that checkmate was unavoidable.

He was wrong! As soon as the game was over, he was shown a perfectly adequate defense that would have saved his position from defeat. But it was too late — he'd already resigned. The game was over.

When it comes to resigning, then, don't be too sure that the situation is hopeless. A bit of skepticism, a bit of "I'm from Missouri" is in order.

Maybe you don't see all there is in the position. Maybe you give your opponent too much credit.

On that score, here's a useful point to keep in mind:

If your opponent is a much better player than you are, a hopeless position is really hopeless.

But suppose the two of you are about equally matched. Suppose you're much the better player? What then?

When Not to Resign

If you and your opponent are about equally matched, a hopeless position may not be so hopeless, after all!

Does your opponent have weak spots in his play? Is he prone to overconfidence or carelessness in winning positions? Perhaps he scares easily, so that a sham threat on your part may throw him off balance.

On the other hand, *if your opponent is much weaker than you,* then even a serious oversight on your part may not justify your resigning the game. Why give him credit for a degree of ability he hasn't demonstrated in the past?

Loss of the Queen — which is fatal against a *good* player — may be quite bearable against a duffer. This is a principle which I learned the hard way.

When I was about fourteen years old I often used to play in ten-second tournaments at the Marshall Chess Club. (In such events the rule is that you can take no more than ten seconds on any move!)

Very often I would be required to give Queen odds — that is, start the game with my Queen removed from the board — against dignified, elderly opponents who had been playing chess before I was born.

I was always appalled to have to spot these players such an enormous handicap. The fact was, though, that they were not very good players. They had no notion of how to exploit their overwhelming material advantage.

After a few moves they would overlook the loss of a piece. Naturally I would capture it and feel a bit relieved.

Then another oversight — and I'd be almost even in material. Then still another blunder, and I'd actually be ahead!

This process happens time and again when we blunder away an important piece against a very weak player. Keep on playing, and you will regain the lost material with interest.

Ripe for Resigning

Now let's see two situations where resignation is called for:

Diagram 8 (*Black to play*)

Black is in check by White's Queen. His King cannot capture the White Queen, as she is guarded by White's Rook.

Black, in fact, has only one move: . . . *King to King*

Rook 1 (. . . K–KR1). But in that case White forces checkmate by *Queen to King Rook 7 check* (Q–KR7 ch) or *Queen to King Knight 7 check* (Q–KN7 ch).

All this, you see, is absolutely forced. Black has no way to avoid checkmate. If he is matched with a strong opponent, resignation is in order.

If White is a weak player, Black might just as well try . . . *King to King Rook 1* (. . . K–KR1). The chance that White will miss the checkmate is a microscopically small one, but it can be tried.

In Diagram 9 it is Black's move. Note that his Queen is attacked:

Diagram 9 (*Black to play*)

BLACK

WHITE

White has played out a Knight to attack Black's Queen.

Black should of course move his Queen out of harm's way. Instead, overlooking the attack on his Queen, he plays . . . *Pawn to King 4???* (. . . P–K4???).

As you've probably guessed, those question marks tell us

that Black has just played a very bad move. White naturally captures the Black Queen with his Knight, remaining with an overwhelming material advantage.

The game has gone only four moves, and Black is a Queen down! Not much point in playing out this one.

By now you probably realize that to enforce checkmate or bring about your opponent's resignation, you will generally have to be considerably ahead in material.

You must therefore be familiar with the values of the different pieces *in relation to each other*.

What those values are, and why they are important, will be shown in the next chapter.

Meanwhile, remember these rules about resigning:

Hold out against weak players!

Don't delay unduly in resigning a hopeless game against a good player!

CHAPTER 3

WHAT'S IT WORTH?

The Values of the Pieces

There is one type of question which turns up repeatedly in my chess classes. A student will say, "Why not play here?" indicating a move that gives up a piece with little or no compensation.

I look puzzled. No matter how often I have this experience, I am never prepared for the thought that a player *does not know the value of each piece*—or else *does not realize that loss of material should lead to loss of the game.*

"Why," I answer finally, "your opponent just captures the piece — like this — and you have nothing to show for it but a check or two."

"Oh well, I don't mind losing the Bishop; it's a lot of fun to see what will happen."

At this stage I have to explain that each of the pieces in a game of chess has a certain value. You cannot afford to lose one of these pieces. You cannot make a gift of a piece to your opponent. If you violate this rule, you ought to lose the game—and very likely you will!

Which brings us to the point of this chapter: *What*

value do you place on each piece, and what do you have to get in return if you part with one of your units?

Even Exchanges

Common sense tells you that you can exchange your Queen for the opponent's Queen, your Bishop for the opponent's Bishop, etc., without losing any material.

Take Diagram 10 as an example:

Diagram 10 (*Black to play*)

BLACK

WHITE

Black's Bishop captures White's Bishop (. . . BxB), and White recaptures with his Queen Bishop Pawn (PxB). This is an even Exchange: Bishop for Bishop.

Again it is Black's move, and now his Rook on the Queen Bishop file captures White's Rook on that file (. . . RxR). White recaptures with his other Rook

(RxR). This is another even Exchange: Rook for Rook. Neither side has gained or lost material by these swaps.

Diagram 11 shows a number of exchanging possibilities. Let's look at two even Exchanges here:

Diagram 11 (*White to play*)

BLACK

WHITE

White starts off by capturing Black's King Pawn with his Queen Pawn (PxP). Black replies by recapturing with his Queen Pawn (. . . PxP). First even Exchange: Pawn for Pawn.

Now it is White's turn again, and he plays *Queen takes Queen check* (QxQch), and Black retakes, either with the Knight on QB3 (. . . NxQ) or with his King (. . . KxQ). Another even Exchange: Queen for Queen.

So much for even Exchanges.

But what about all those puzzling questions like:

Can I swap my Queen for his Rook?

Is a Bishop stronger than a Knight?
Is a Rook more valuable than a Bishop?
Is a Knight worth three Pawns?

Relative Values

In order to provide you with a rough-and-ready answer
to all such questions, here is a table of standard values:

QUEEN	9 points
ROOK	5 points
BISHOP	3 points
KNIGHT	3 points
PAWN	1 point

(What about the King? We don't assign him any value
in this table because checkmate automatically ends the
game. If you want to be mathematical about it, you might
say the King's value is equal to infinity! And if you're
checkmated, your King's value is equal to zero.)

By looking at this table, we can answer the questions
that baffle many players. For example:

The Queen (value — 9 points) should *not* be swapped
for a Rook (value — 5 points).

A Bishop (value — 3 points) and a Knight (value — 3
points) are equal in value.

A Rook (value — 5 points) is worth more than a Bishop
(value — 3 points).

A Knight (value — 3 points) is worth three Pawns (value — 3 points).

In the overwhelming majority of cases you will find this table a highly dependable guide. You can apply it successfully even if you have no idea how these values were derived. But if you are curious about this, here's one way to get an insight into the values of the pieces:

Cruising Range

Using an empty board, place a Queen on one of the four center squares. How many squares can the Queen move to? Count them up, and you will find that she has a choice of moving to no less than 27 of the 63 empty squares. This is a phenomenal range, and shows what the Queen can accomplish with its power of moving horizontally, vertically and diagonally.

Now place a Rook *anywhere* on an empty board. No matter where the Rook is posted, it has a choice of 14 possible squares to move to. This adds up to a lot of power — even if it is only about half of what the Queen can accomplish. The Rook cannot move diagonally, but it *can* move horizontally and vertically, and it reaches squares of both colors.

How about the Bishop? On the empty board, the Bishop has a maximum of 13 squares it can reach, and a minimum of 8. (It all depends on where you place the Bishop.)

The Knight is quite effective *in the center zone,* having a choice of 8 moves there. (On the side squares at the edge of the board its mobility is radically scaled down. In fact, a Knight on a corner square can make only 2 moves. Try it and see.)

The "Lowly" Pawn

The Pawn has the least value of all the chessmen. It can move only one square at a time (except when it is still on its home square). It has no backward-moving power. It has only two capturing possibilities.

These factors explain why the Pawn is rated the humblest of the chess units — and why inexperienced players despise the Pawn.

This is a pity. Most players are apt to throw away a Pawn or two — or three — without a care. But that is poor policy, because the Pawn has a remarkable power possessed by no other chess unit. *The Pawn is able in certain cases to promote to a Queen or Rook or Bishop or Knight.* (More about this on pages 81–96.)

Because every Pawn is a potential Queen, you should treat it with more respect than you have probably done in the past. Proper attention to the Pawn's promotion powers can make you a much stronger player.

Another valuable aspect of Pawn play is this: the very weakness of the Pawn is sometimes a paradoxical element of strength! Because the Pawn is worth less than any of the other units, they have to run away from the Pawn's attack, unless they can capture it at once.

More Comparative Values

Now let's draw some more useful conclusions from the table of values. The Queen (value — 9 points) is worth more than a Rook plus Bishop or Knight (total value — 8 points). Queen against Rook plus Bishop or Knight plus Pawn (total value — 9 points) is about an equal fight.

Two Rooks are definitely worth more than the Queen. However, inexperienced players may have trouble in maneuvering the Rooks for combined operations. It takes skill and experience to make the Rooks work together.

Bishop vs. Knight

What about the age-old question of Bishop vs. Knight? The average player fears the Knight's hopping powers, which seem to promise ugly surprises. On the other hand, masters will often tell you that the Bishop is more effective than the Knight.

As far as most of us are concerned, the Bishop and Knight are equal in value. The Bishop gets around faster,

but it is limited to squares of one color. The Knight takes
more time to reach a distant part of the board, but he moves
from a black square to a white one, or from a white square
to a black one. This means that sooner or later he can
reach every square on the board, regardless of color.

The moral is, then, that exchanging Bishop for Knight,
or Knight for Bishop, is an even Exchange. Let's see how
this works out in Diagram 11 (page 37).

Assume that it's White's move and his Queen Pawn
captures Black's King Pawn (PxP). Black takes the White
Bishop with his Queen Knight Pawn (. . . PxB). Mo-
mentarily Black has won a piece for a measly Pawn.

But now White's advanced Pawn captures Black's
Knight at King Bishop 3 (PxN). This is an even Exchange: White has parted with a Bishop and captured
a Knight. Or put the other way round: Black has parted
with a Knight and captured a Bishop.

However, two Bishops have a bit of advantage if opposed by a Bishop and Knight. Two Bishops are even
more of an advantage if they are opposed by two Knights.

When the two Bishops are working well together, all
the squares on the board—white and black—are within
their range. In such cases, as you might suspect, their
scope is considerable.

The standard checkmate with the two Bishops (Diagram 12) is a good example of the power of the combined
Bishops, especially on the open board. White gives check
by playing the white-squared Bishop to King Knight 2
(B–N2ch); and this is actually checkmate!

Diagram 12 (*White to play*)

BLACK

WHITE

Note how White's co-operating long-range Bishops reach across the whole board to "put the finger" on Black's lone King.

Inexperienced players are often unclear about the difference in value between a Rook and a Bishop (or Knight). To repeat: the Rook has a value of 5 points. A Bishop or Knight is valued at 3 points.

The moral is clear: Don't part with one of your Rooks for an enemy Bishop or Knight. But if you can capture an enemy Rook in return for your own Bishop or Knight, then by all means do so.

If you lose a Rook in return for a Bishop or Knight, you're said to "lose the Exchange" — in other words, you're on the short end of the Exchange.

If, however, you capture a Rook in return for your own Bishop or Knight, you "win the Exchange."

Note that a Rook (value — 5 points) is worth more than a Bishop or Knight plus a Pawn (total value — 4 points).

But match a Rook (value — 5 points) against a Bishop or Knight plus two Pawns (total value — 5 points) and there you have material equality.

Let's see how this works out in actual play (Diagram 13). As the position stands, White has a Rook for a Bishop and two Pawns. Black is the Exchange down, as we say, but he is two Pawns ahead. Material is therefore even.

However, if we remove one of the Black Pawns, then Black has only one Pawn for the Exchange and is behind in material. Remove still another Black Pawn and Black is a clear Exchange down.

Diagram 13

BLACK

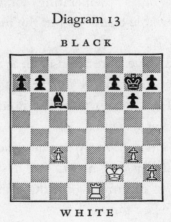

WHITE

Winning Material

As you've seen in Chapter 2, winning material should lead to checkmate. Now that you know the values of the

pieces, you are in a better position to appreciate the importance of making a net profit in capturing.

Diagram 14 illustrates the point:

Diagram 14 *(White to play)*

BLACK

WHITE

White plays his Knight from the King 2 square (K2) to King Bishop 4 (KB4) attacking Black's Queen. After this move (N–KB4) Black's Queen is lost no matter what he does.

His best move is to capture White's Rook (. . . QxRch). But then White's Knight at King Knight 3 (KN3) captures the Queen (NxQ) and Black has lost his Queen (value — 9 points) in return for the White Rook (value — 5 points). Black should lose the game.

Even the best of us can lose material through inattention. José Capablanca, a former World Champion, once found that he was forced to lose a piece as early as the ninth move because of his careless play. Did he resign? Not at all! He fought on for 54 moves before giving up.

However, all his hard work was wasted. One careless move, and his game was compromised! Of course, he may have held out only because no one likes to resign — especially at a very early stage. It was said of Capa that when he had to resign, he did it "with the hauteur of a millionaire giving a dime to a beggar." In that way, perhaps, he softened the sting of losing.

With a good grasp of the values of the chess pieces, we can now proceed to learn methods of getting the most work out of our chess units.

The next three chapters describe ways of rendering our opponent powerless by certain kinds of raiding attacks. *These are the techniques of winning material and thereby laying the groundwork for checkmating your opponent.*

CHAPTER 4

THE THREE STRONGEST MOVES

1. *Checks*

Here's an interesting experiment to try on your chess-playing friends.

As you know, it's customary to announce "Check!" whenever you check your opponent's King. However, such announcement is not required by the rules.

Now for the experiment. *Try giving check without announcing it.* You will be amazed — and entertained — at the frequency with which your opponents will overlook that they are in check.

The point is this: most players are so lacking in alertness that they overlook the most important fact in the game of chess. That most important fact is a *check* — an attack on the King.

Chess players often complain that in any given position they don't know what to do; they don't know what to look for.

Here, then, is the first thing to look for: "Am I in check? "Am I giving check?

"Am I in a position to give check?

"Is he in a position to give check?"

If the answer to any one of these questions is "Yes!" then you have a goal, an indicator, a hint as to what you must think about and how you must proceed.

A check, you see, is peremptory and menacing. *It cannot be ignored.* As explained in the first chapter, something must be done about it. Either the checking piece must be captured; or the checked King must move; or the checked King must be shielded from attack.

Because the check is peremptory, it frequently enables us to win material. If you watch for the right opportunities, you will see how the *priority of check* enables you to win material.

Priority of Check

Before we go on to practical examples, let's be clear about what we mean by *priority of check.*

When you threaten the King with a check and menace something else at the same time, your opponent must above all guard against the check. The *priority of check* may inflict a crushing loss of material on him.

In Diagram 15 White plays *Queen to Queen Rook 4 check* (Q–QR4ch). This is a check, and more than a check: it also attacks Black's Bishop at his Queen Knight 5 square (QN5). But Black, subject to the *priority of check,*

Diagram 15 (*White to play*)

must parry the attack on his King, and thus he must lose the Bishop!

Forking Check

Diagram 16 shows a stratagem that you will find most profitable. Black's Queen is attacked by White's Bishop on the King Knight 5 square (KN5). Instead of trying to save his valuable Queen, Black plays a move that looks idiotic.

He plays . . . *Queen takes Bishop* (. . . QxB). Naturally White replies with *Queen takes Queen* (QxQ). As Black has given up his Queen for only a Bishop, you might conclude that he has a hopelessly lost game. In most cases you would be right, but not here.

For now Black plays . . . *Knight to King Bishop 6*

Diagram 16 (*Black to play*)

BLACK

WHITE

check (. . . N–KB6ch). This attacks White's King and Queen—or, as we say of such Knight moves, it forks the King and Queen.

White would of course be delighted to move his Queen to a safe spot — but this is out of the question. The inexorable *priority of check* forces him to attend to his King's safety.

After the White King moves — and he *must* move — Black captures the White Queen (. . . NxQ). Now, if you review this transaction, you will find that Black made a sham "sacrifice" of his Queen and won a Bishop. The technique for gaining material was a check — a forking check.

A check also does the trick in Diagram 17. Black has two Rooks for two Bishops, which is quite a material advantage. But White's *Bishop to King Knight 7 check* (B–KN7ch) spells disaster for Black.

Diagram 17 *(White to play)*

BLACK

WHITE

Why? If Black doesn't take the Bishop, he loses his Queen with no compensation whatever.

On the other hand, if Black does capture the Bishop (. . . KxB), then his King no longer protects his Queen, and White replies *Queen takes Queen check* (QxQch) with a decisive material advantage.

Again *priority of check* has left the defender without resource. He has to save his King, and leave his poor Queen to her gruesome fate.

Removing the Defender

Another valuable winning technique is seen in Diagram 18. We call this method of attack "removing the defender."

White plays the deadly *Bishop takes Knight check* (BxNch), sawing off the Black Queen's protection.

Diagram 18 (*White to play*)

BLACK

WHITE

Naturally Black would like to save his Queen; but **the** *priority of check* makes that impossible. He must get out of check, with the result that he loses his Queen. This is one of the most frequently used winning techniques. Opportunities to use it come up very often in practical play, and you will find it useful to be familiar with this winning method.

Diagram 19 illustrates still another method of exploiting *priority of check*.

White plays *Bishop to Queen Bishop 4 check* (B–QB4 ch). White is not only checking; he has *uncovered an attack* by the White Queen on the Black Queen. (We call this type of attack "discovered attack.")

Black can answer this check in various ways; but no matter what he does, his loss of material will be so heavy that he might just as well resign right now. One judicious check and Black has nothing left to play for!

Diagram 19 (*White to play*)

By now your batting eye for checks and checking moves ought to be sharpened quite a bit. At the beginning of this chapter we emphasized the need for looking out for checks. Let's go a step further. We want to look not only for checks, but for checks that contain an additional threat.

When you check your opponent, you coerce him. You *limit his replies* to some sort of move that gets rid of the check. If you can combine the check with an additional threat, so much the better.

What you are doing is this: *in one single move you double your attacking potential and at the same time greatly narrow down your opponent's choice of defensive action.*

Take Diagram 20 as a very simple example. White is giving check with his Bishop. (The Bishop is of course immune to capture, being guarded by White's Rook.)

Priority of check deprives Black of any defense against this "skewer" attack. He *must* move his King, allowing

Diagram 20 (*Black to play*)

BLACK

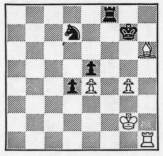

WHITE

White to play *Bishop takes Rook* (BxR). Thus White has forced the win of the Exchange, leaving him with a Rook against a Knight. This is a sure win for White.

Again, in Diagram 21 White has reason to gnash his teeth over the *priority of check.*

As the position stands, White is ahead in material. But

Diagram 21 (*Black to play*)

BLACK

WHITE

now comes the nasty check . . . *Bishop to Queen Bishop 4 check* (. . . B–QB4ch).

This exposes White's Queen to a "discovered attack" by the Black Rook. (This situation, by the way, reminds us very much of Diagram 19.) White would like nothing better than to save his Queen, but his job is to get out of check. Result: he loses his Queen with no compensation whatever.

The "Discovered" Check

Turn to Diagram 22, which introduces a special kind of check: the "discovered check." This type of check comes about when Piece A moves and thereby uncovers (or "discovers") a check by Piece B.

Diagram 22 (*Black to play*)

BLACK

WHITE

In Diagram 22, the Black Bishop on King Knight 4 (KN4) moves and thereby creates a discovered check by the Black Queen. This type of check can have a terrific impact if you apply yourself to get the most power out of it.

The Black Bishop has eight different squares to play to in order to give discovered check. The best move is . . . *Bishop to King 6 discovered check* (. . . B–K6 dis ch).

Why is this best? Because it not only attacks White's King; it also attacks — doubly! — White's Knight on the King Bishop 2 square (KB2). No matter how White plays, he must lose the doubly menaced Knight.

Double Check

Sometimes the piece that uncovers a discovered check also gives check as well. This involves a "double check," about which you want to notice two things.

The first is that the only way to answer a double check is to move your King — if you can. The second is that the double check is one of the deadliest weapons in chess.

In Diagram 23, for example, White has a terrific attack against the exposed Black King. Just what is the finishing touch that puts Black's King out of his misery?

White can give a discovered check by moving his Bishop, but Black has a winning reply in . . . *Bishop takes Queen* (. . . BxQ).

Hence a discovered check won't do — or will it? The

Diagram 23 (*White to play*)

right way is *Bishop to King Knight 7 double check* (B–KN7 dbl ch).

Now Black cannot capture the Queen because he is also in check from the White Bishop. All that remains is . . . *King takes Bishop* (. . . KxB). But then comes *Rook to King Bishop 7 checkmate* (R–KB7 mate).

Diagram 24 (*Black to play*)

For the last example in this chapter we have a really devastating double check (Diagram 24).

Black plays . . . *Bishop to Queen Bishop 6 double check* (. . . B–QB6 dbl ch).

White cannot capture the Black Queen because the Black Bishop is *also* giving check! Nor can White capture the Black Bishop because the Black Queen is also giving check! Nor can White move his King out of check. In fact, he is checkmated!

These ten examples of check have hammered away at the theme that while all checks are dangerous to the King, many checks are dangerous to other pieces as well.

So far we have seen how a check may be combined with another threat. Now we proceed to another type of attack which is found far more often: *attacks without check.*

"They've been trying to decide for the past twenty minutes whether to walk uptown or downtown."

CHAPTER 5

THE THREE STRONGEST MOVES

2. *Capturing Threats*

Have you ever noticed how an unexpected capture can immediately decide the fate of a game?

Even first-class masters may underestimate the strength of a capture. Where the capture has a most unlikely look about it, they may miss the possibility of the capture altogether.

Diagram 25 (*Black to play*)

BLACK

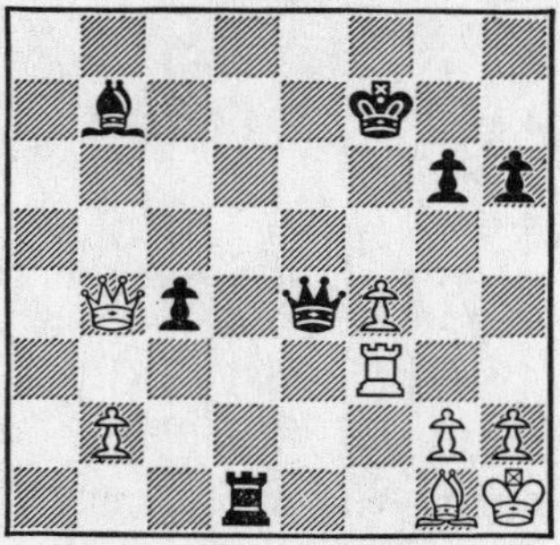

WHITE

One of the most drastic examples I know of occurred in the London Tournament of 1951, the most important international tournament of that year. Scheltinga, a leading Dutch master, had won a Pawn from Alexander, England's outstanding player.

White's pieces are somewhat tied up but he seems quite safe. There is an ominous detail, quite overlooked by White, in that his Queen is way off to the side instead of playing an active role in the game.

Imagine the shock to White when his opponent plays . . . *Queen takes Rook* (. . . QxR)!

White has to resign after this loss of his Rook, the point being that if he plays *Pawn takes Queen* (PxQ), Black replies . . . *Bishop takes Pawn* (. . . BxP) mate!

Captures, as you see from this example, can be almost as deadly as many types of checks. So we consider captures — and the threat of captures — among the outstandingly strong moves on the board. Captures, like checks, decide the fate of many a game.

How to Win Material

Captures are of two kinds — even Exchanges and all other kinds.

When you capture your opponent's Queen and he captures yours in return, we have an even Exchange. When your opponent captures one of your Pawns, and you capture one of his in return, that is another kind of even Exchange.

If one player captures a Bishop and the other captures a Knight, that is still an even Exchange. For these pieces have the same value. (See page 41.)

However, in this chapter we're interested in the other kind of captures — *the kind that wins material for one player and loses material for the other.*

If you capture an opposing unit without losing one of your own, *you win material.* Or, if you capture an opposing unit and give up a unit of your own of lesser value, *you still win material.*

How deeply ingrained capturing is in the mind of a chess master can be seen from this story. Blackburne, the great English nineteenth-century master, often went on tours when he would give a series of simultaneous exhibitions. In the course of these exhibitions he would take on anywhere from twenty to fifty opponents at the same time.

At one such exhibition one of Blackburne's hard-pressed opponents ordered a drink for himself to relax a bit. When the drink arrived, he set it at the side of his board while he pondered his move. As Blackburne arrived at the table, he saw the drink, assumed it had been ordered for him, picked it up, and finished it off at one gulp. He won that game very quickly.

Later in the evening someone asked Blackburne what had happened at that particular table. "Why, nothing remarkable," he replied. "My opponent left a glass of whisky *en prise;* I captured it *en passant,* and won easily!"

To be "capture-minded" is second nature to the chess master because having an advantage in material is one of the likeliest ways to win a game.

Advantage in material is the chief factor that helps you enforce checkmate or promote a Pawn to Queen.

(If you do not have the values of the pieces firmly fixed in mind, you ought to refer to them now on page 38 before you go any further in this chapter.)

Removing the Defender

Diagram 26 shows a position in which many a player would fail to see the possibility of winning material:

Diagram 26 (*White to play*)

BLACK

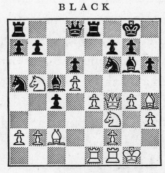

WHITE

The right move for White is *Bishop takes Knight* (BxN).

Black has to capture the Bishop, and he has two ways of doing it — with his King Knight Pawn or with his Queen.

If he takes the Bishop with his Pawn (. . . PxB), then White can answer *Queen takes King Rook Pawn* (QxKRP). In the positions held in Diagram 26 it would have been a frightful blunder for White to have taken the King Rook Pawn with his Queen as his first move. For then Black would have replied . . . *Pawn takes Queen* (. . . PxQ).

On the other hand if Black retakes with his Queen instead of his Pawn . . . *Queen takes Bishop* (. . . QxB), White plays *Queen takes Queen* (QxQ) followed by *Knight to Queen Bishop 7* forcing the win of a Black Rook in return for White's Knight. This would be a distinct gain of material for White. It is known, you will recall, as winning the Exchange. (See page 43.)

Note that in the positions held in Diagram 26, White could not play *Knight to Queen Bishop 7* (N–QB7) directly, for then the Black Queen could simply capture the foolhardy Knight.

This points up the fact that the winning technique used here by White is called "removing the defender." If Black recaptures with his Pawn, he loses a Pawn. If he recaptures with his Queen, he loses the Exchange.

"Removing the defender" is a valuable winning method that you can use repeatedly once you are familiar with it. You will find that a check or a capture is often the prelude to removing the defender, after which you can win material to your heart's content.

Let's see how this method works in Diagram 27:

Diagram 27 (*White to play*)

BLACK

WHITE

White, to be sure, can play *Bishop takes Knight* (BxN). But Black simply recaptures: . . . *Rook takes Bishop* (. . . RxB). No profit there.

Let's carry the process a step further: White plays *Rook takes Rook* (RxR), and Black replies . . . *Queen takes Rook* (. . . QxR). No profit there either; just two even Exchanges.

Should we conclude, then, that White cannot win material in the position of Diagram 27? That conclusion would be hasty; *what we need is a preparatory threat to drive away a defender.*

The right way to start in the position of Diagram 27 is *Knight to Queen Rook 4* (N–QR4). This attacks Black's Queen.

Study the position carefully and you will see that the Black Queen, now under attack, cannot move to a square where it continues to guard the Black Knight at the Queen 3 square.

Thus, if Black retreats . . . *Queen to Queen Rook 2* (. . . Q–QR2), White simply captures the Knight with his Rook or Bishop, and he has won a whole piece — a winning advantage.

But Black isn't licked — not yet, anyway. He can make a fight of it in this way:

He plays . . . *Queen takes Queen Knight Pawn* (. . . QxQNP). Black thus puts the White Queen under attack, and he figures that after White plays *Queen takes Queen* (QxQ), he will reply . . . *Knight takes Queen* (. . . NxQ); all danger will be over for him.

It does seem, as we study Diagram 28, that Black is out of all his troubles:

Diagram 28 (*White to play*)

BLACK

WHITE

However, White can say, "We planned it that way," for he now proceeds with *Rook takes Rook* (RxR).

Black replies . . . *Rook takes Rook* (. . . RxR). He has no choice.

Now White continues with *Bishop takes Knight* (BxN). Black's miserable Knight has no protection; Black has no recapture; White has won a clear piece.

What happened? Black tried the only defense he could find, and he did succeed in saving his menaced Knight on the Queen 3 square, but unfortunately, in the course of a series of captures, the defense of his *other* Knight became unhinged. Result: Black has lost a piece in return for a mere Pawn, and he will lose the game.

Sometimes, as in Diagram 29, it is fairly easy to see a chance for a killing capture. This is particularly true when a capture threatens a decisive check.

Diagram 29 (*Black to play*)

BLACK

WHITE

Black can play . . . *Knight to King 7 check* (. . . N–K7ch) with a view to forking White's King and Queen. Nice work, you think, until you notice that White can simply capture the Knight with his Bishop now on the Queen 3 square. Too bad!

Instead of dropping the idea, however, let's look for captures. White's Bishop on the Queen 3 square is the defender.

Well, suppose Black removes the defender?

How?

By playing . . . *Rook takes Bishop* (. . . RxB).

After this capture White is lost. If he captures Black's Rook, then the nasty Knight check forks White's King and Queen. On the other hand, if White guards against this threat, Black's Rook escapes capture and Black has won a clear piece, with a won game.

In Diagram 30 White does not rely on a checking possibility, but his method is forceful all the same:

Diagram 30 (*White to play*)

BLACK

WHITE

Most players would see nothing wrong with Black's game, but there is a sad flaw in it:

His Rook on the King 1 square guards his Bishop and also his other Rook.

What of it? Just this: we distrust positions in which one piece has to protect two or more. It makes too much work for the defender.

In the position of Diagram 30 a White Rook attacks Black's Bishop; the White Queen attacks a Black Rook.

To get the most advantage out of the situation, White plays *Rook takes Bishop* (RxB).

Now the fat is in the fire as far as Black is concerned. If he replies . . . *Rook takes Rook* (. . . RxR), he leaves his other Rook in the lurch, allowing *Queen takes Rook check* (QxRch) and White has won a clear piece.

Thus, after White captures the Bishop he forces the win of a piece no matter what Black does. Again and again you see in these examples the profitable ways of winning material which are generally overlooked by most players.

In Diagram 31 the winning method is tantalizingly difficult — or tantalizingly simple, depending on how you look at it:

Diagram 31 (*White to play*)

BLACK

WHITE

White's Queen attacks Black's Bishop, which in turn is defended by Black's Queen. Of course, it would be a huge blunder on White's part to capture the Bishop, losing his Queen for only a Bishop.

But it's just at this point, where you mutter, "No dice!" that you really have to apply yourself.

If Black's Bishop were guarded by a Pawn, that would be solid protection and you could forget about trying to capture the Bishop. But when the Bishop is defended by a piece, the defense *may* turn out to be unstable.

And in fact the defense IS unstable, if you turn your glance to the Queen-side and see the explosive power unleashed by the quiet *Pawn to Queen Knight 4* (P–QN4). Why this move?

Black's Knight is attacked by the White Pawn and must move.

Once the Black Knight moves, White plays *Rook takes Rook* (RxR) with a winning game! Black, to be sure, can reply . . . *Queen takes Rook* (. . . QxR). But in that case his Queen no longer defends his Bishop, and White can reply *Queen takes Bishop* (QxB), winning a clear piece.

Thus the advance of White's Queen Knight Pawn made it possible for him to *remove the defender*. But, you may say, "It's easy for a master to see these possibilities. It's not so easy to find these moves."

True; but you have a very important principle to guide you. *If you are attacking,* as White is attacking in Diagram 31, *you at least have the possibility of a winning capture.*

"I hate to interrupt, gentlemen, but you both won twenty minutes ago."

Threat or attack is the key to winning captures; for the player on the defensive there is no immediate capturing opportunity. But an existing attack, even if your opponent has apparently parried it, still holds out the hope that you can make the attack irresistible.

The "Double Attack"

Another way of almost infallibly guaranteeing winning captures is the "double attack." Diagram 32 is a good example:

Diagram 32 (*White to play*)

BLACK

WHITE

Here the double attack is *Pawn to King 5* (P–K5). We call this kind of move a "Pawn fork," as the Pawn threatens to capture the Black Queen and also the Black Knight at his King Bishop 3 square.

(All "forks" are double attacks.)

Of course Black cannot dream of capturing this cocky Pawn, as it is guarded by the White Queen. So Black has no choice: he must save his Queen by retreating that piece, looking on helplessly while White captures the Knight.

Double attacks are among the most frequent attacks in chess, and among the most effective. For here *one unit attacks two hostile units at the same time*. What could be more devastating — and economical?

The same idea turns up in Diagram 33 in somewhat more elaborate form:

Diagram 33 (*Black to play*)

BLACK

WHITE

Black's Queen attacks White's Knight at the King 4 square, but the Knight is amply guarded by White's Queen at the King 2 square.

Does that mean that Black can accomplish nothing at all here? By no means.

As we saw previously, while there's attack there's hope. Black's attack is parried *for the time being;* but isn't there some way he can strengthen that attack and make it work? Yes: . . . *Rook to King Bishop 5* (. . . R–KB5).

This attacks White's Knight *a second time*. It also attacks White's Bishop, which is *unguarded*.

This double attack is too much for White. He can save his Knight, but only at the cost of losing his Bishop. He can save his Bishop at the cost of losing his Knight. But he cannot save the Bishop AND the Knight! There you see the cruel effectiveness of the double attack.

The crushing effectiveness of the double attack has still another virtue: it enables you to calculate a whole series of moves in advance. Diagram 34 is a good example:

Diagram 34 (*Black to play*)

BLACK

WHITE

Black attacks White's Bishop twice (with Queen and Rook). White defends this Bishop twice (also with Queen and Rook). But somewhere along the line the powerful fork . . . *Knight to King 7 check* (. . . N–K7ch) can play a role.

Actually, Black can win in this position in a number of ways. We shall choose the simplest method.

Black starts off with . . . *Rook takes Bishop* (. . . RxB). White replies *Queen takes Rook* (QxR).

Black now plays . . . *Queen takes Queen* (. . . QxQ) and White replies *Rook takes Queen,* giving us the position of Diagram 35:

Diagram 35 (*Black to play*)

BLACK

WHITE

What has Black accomplished? He has lost the Exchange by giving up his Rook for White's Bishop. Is that all there is to it?

But now comes the stinger, which Black foresaw all along: . . . *Knight to King 7 check* (. . . N–K7ch). White must move his King, whereupon Black captures the White Rook.

The result of the wholesale captures is that Black has won a whole piece. (Count up the remaining pieces on the board to make sure you follow this.)

Black was able to calculate three moves deep because White's moves were *forced*. That is one of the virtues of captures. Since your opponent must recapture in order to maintain material equality, you can foresee his reply and thus calculate a forced line of play.

Of course, it was the forking check at the end that made Black's calculation sound. This is the way Black's mind worked in the position of Diagram 34: first he saw the possibility of the Knight check and then he searched for a sequence of moves that *would make the check work*. This type of thinking is very common in chess.

In cases like this one you might compare a chess player to the author of a whodunit who starts his work by figuring out the solution which will come at the end of his book. In Diagram 34 the Knight's forking check is the "solution." Black's task, once he sees this check, is to search for the moves that make the check meaningful.

Pinning Attacks

Diagram 36 illustrates a method of winning material based on a pin.

We say a chess unit is pinned when it is unable to move off the line on which it is placed. Thus, in Diagram 36, when White plays *Pawn to Queen Knight 4* (P–QN4) Black must not reply . . . *Pawn takes Pawn* (. . . PxP), for this would lose his Queen.

Diagram 36 (*White to play*)

BLACK

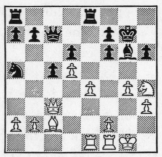

WHITE

Black's Queen Bishop Pawn, then, is pinned: it does not dare move off the Queen Bishop file.

But Black's Knight is attacked. No matter where it moves, it will be captured. Thus Black must lose a piece because of the pin. (In Chapter 10 we will find many striking examples of the power of the pin.)

From what you have now learned about captures and capturing threats, you can see why captures are among the strongest moves on the board.

Look for capturing possibilities; see how you can combine them with checks; watch out for enemy units that have to protect other enemy units; look for possibilities of double attack; note opportunities for forking and pinning.

These are the moves that win games. To be familiar with them, to be able to pick them out of an otherwise meaningless position, to use them, to crush your opponent — these are the marks of a winning player.

You still need to learn about the third type of strong move — the transformation of the "measly" Pawn into a Queen that gives you an overwhelming material advantage. This subject is treated in the next chapter.

CHAPTER 6

THE THREE STRONGEST MOVES

3. *Pawn Promotion*

If you've ever been inside a chess club, you're familiar with what sounds like "two husky workingmen alternately and enthusiastically beating a two-inch oak plank with wooden mallets, the sequence of the blows and volume of racket rapidly rising in increasing crescendo."

Why does the noise get louder and louder? Very simple. Two players are each racing to queen a Pawn. Who will queen first? Neither one knows, and they're too excited to count. So the players bang the Pawns down as they advance them tensely to the respective queening square.

These players are not world champions, and they never will be. But one thing they do know thoroughly, and that is:

The queening power of a Pawn is one of the mightiest weapons on the chessboard.

That is why we rank Pawn promotion among the three strongest kinds of moves.

The Power of Pawn Promotion

Few of us have ever stopped to realize that successful queening of a Pawn is equivalent to winning an enormous amount of material. By queening a Pawn you can often accomplish one or more of the following results:

1. Mate your opponent on the spot.
2. Be a whole Queen ahead in material, making it imperative for your opponent to resign.
3. Win a Rook or Bishop or Knight, after which your quick victory is almost one hundred per cent certain.
4. Turn overwhelming material inferiority into overwhelming material superiority.
5. Tie down important enemy pieces to hold back the Pawn which is on the point of queening.

Quite a formidable showing for the "measly" Pawn, isn't it?

The Pawn is the only unit on the chessboard that has the power of promoting to a unit of much greater value.

Once the Pawn reaches the eighth rank — the farthest row on the board — you have your choice of promoting it to a Queen, a Rook, a Bishop, or a Knight. Naturally the Queen, as the strongest piece of all, is our usual choice.

(There are some situations in which it is advisable to promote to a Rook, a Knight, or a Bishop. Such "underpromotion" may be necessary to avoid stalemate, which is explained on page 184. However, such positions are much too rare to require extended study.)

A Pawn Gives Checkmate!

You may be startled by the statement that a Pawn can bring about checkmate in one single move. The position in Diagram 37 offers the proof:

Diagram 37 (*Black to play*)

BLACK

WHITE

Material is even. But the question here is not how much material, but what kind of material. Black's Queen Pawn is a priceless asset that decides the game at once.

Black plays . . . *Pawn to Queen 8 (becoming a Queen) check* — or . . . P–Q8(Q)ch. Diagram 38 shows what has happened.

Black's advanced Pawn is transformed into a Queen. The new Queen is giving check. White's King has no escape. *White is checkmated.*

This is an example of the sledgehammer power that goes into Pawn promotion. And note this, too:

In Diagram 37, material was even. But one little Pawn move leads to Diagram 38, where Black is a Queen ahead!

Diagram 38 (*Final position*)

BLACK

WHITE

Promotion by Capture

Now turn to Diagram 39 — an example of queening in an actual game.

To appreciate this example, you have to remember that a Pawn can queen not only by direct advance. *It can also queen by capturing* — in the orthodox manner of Pawn capture.

In the position of Diagram 39, for example, White's advanced Queen Pawn cannot move down to the last row. Its promotion is blocked by a sturdy Black Rook.

Yet despite this obstacle White wins handsomely with *Rook to King 8 check* (R–K8ch).

Diagram 39 (*White to play*)

Black's reply is forced: . . . *Rook takes Rook* (. . . RxR). Now White can capture the Black Rook either way and win.

Let us suppose that White's second move is *Rook takes Rook check* (RxRch).

Black's reply is again forced: . . . *Rook takes Rook* (. . . RxR). This brings us to Diagram 40:

Diagram 40 (*White to play*)

White plays *Pawn takes Rook* (*becoming a Queen*) *check* — or PxR(Q)ch. Again it is checkmate. The mouse-like Pawn has grown into a Frankenstein monster which forces Black's immediate downfall.

Remove the Blockader!

In Diagram 41 White confronts Black with a terrible alternative:

Diagram 41 (*White to play*)

BLACK

WHITE

Material is even, but the decisive factor here is White's powerful King Pawn, blocked by Black's Queen from queening. (Incidentally, what a menial job for Black's Queen — to ride herd on a mere Pawn!)

White plays *Knight to Queen 6* (N–Q6), and Black can resign at once. Why?

His Queen is attacked, and must move. Once the Black Queen moves, White's King Pawn advances to the eighth rank, becoming a Queen and giving check.

Black's Queen captures the new White Queen. (Black has no choice in the matter.) This gives us the position of Diagram 42:

Diagram 42 (*White to play*)

BLACK

WHITE

White now plays *Rook takes Queen check* (RxQch). It is checkmate!

But even if Black's King had some avenue of escape, he would still be quite lost. In effect, the queening of White's advanced Pawn puts him a Queen ahead.

How Pawn Promotion Wins Material

It often happens that when you obtain a new Queen you can hold on to this new piece and have an enormous advantage in material.

"Sorry about the noise. But my husband is celebrating. He queened his first pawn."

At other times — as in the position of Diagram 41 — the new Queen is captured, but at fearful cost. Diagram 43 shows a simple and convincing example of this point at an advanced endgame stage:

Diagram 43 (*White to play*)

BLACK

WHITE

White is "only" a Pawn ahead — but what a Pawn!

It is already at the seventh rank, ready to queen. White plays *Pawn to King 8 (becoming a Queen)* — or P–K8(Q).

Black has no choice: he captures the new Queen with his Rook, and White plays *Rook takes Rook* (RxR).

To sum up what has happened, take a look at Diagram 44.

Comparing Diagram 43 with Diagram 44 as a "before and after" tableau, you can see what has happened:

Black managed to dispose of the new Queen — *but* only at the cost of leaving White a Rook ahead. White will be able to force checkmate in less than eight moves.

Diagram 44 (*Black to play*)

BLACK

WHITE

In Diagram 45 White wins important material in the same fashion as in Diagram 41:

Diagram 45 (*White to play*)

BLACK

WHITE

White's far-advanced Queen Bishop Pawn, poised to queen, gives White the whip hand.

Black's Rook stands on the queening square, preventing the promotion of the menacing White Pawn.

White proceeds on the principle of "Remove the block-ader!" (as in Diagram 41). The decisive move is *Knight to Queen Rook 7* (N–QR7).

This move points a pistol at Black. If he moves his at-tacked Rook — and what else can he do? — then the far-advanced Pawn moves to the eighth rank and becomes a Queen.

Black must then capture the new Queen with his Rook. This leads to the situation on Diagram 46:

Diagram 46 (*White to play*)

BLACK

WHITE

Now White captures the Black Rook with his own Rook or Knight. As in Diagram 44, White is left with a Rook to the good as a result of the queening operations.

As a general proposition, we may say that the pieces of lesser value—Bishop or Knight—are the best blockaders of passed Pawns. The more valuable the blockader, the more vulnerable he is. This sounds paradoxical, but see Dia-gram 41, where the Black Queen is helpless.

Watch for Passed Pawns

Of course it doesn't require an eagle eye to see the power of the far-advanced Pawn by the time it has reached the seventh rank. To recognize the potentialities of a "passed Pawn" is really the hallmark of a good player. Take Diagram 47 as an example:

Diagram 47 (*White to play*)

BLACK

WHITE

White's King Bishop Pawn is a "passed Pawn." So is his Queen Rook Pawn. What makes them "passed Pawns"?

We say a Pawn is passed *when it no longer has opposing Pawns on neighboring files that are capable of capturing it as it advances toward the queening square.*

So here you have a valuable hint for improving your winning technique. When you have a passed Pawn, you have a *candidate for queening.* Such a Pawn should be guarded carefully, nursed along, and gradually advanced toward the queening square.

When you look at a position like the one in Diagram 40, bear in mind that the passed Pawn took quite a while to get to the seventh rank. It started its career at the Queen 2 square. Then it advanced, one move at a time, to Q4, to Q5, to Q6, and finally to Q7.

Now back to Diagram 47.

White's passed Queen Rook Pawn is harmless right now. It's still on its original square.

White's other passed Pawn, the King Bishop Pawn, is another story. By playing *Pawn to King Bishop 7* (P–KB7), White forces an immediate decision.

Black's attacked Rook must move, whereupon the well-protected Pawn advances to the eighth rank, becoming a Queen.

Black must capture the new White Queen with his Rook. White in turn pounces on the Black Rook and remains a Rook ahead. White has an overwhelming material advantage, and Black can save himself further grief by resigning on the spot.

Pawn Promotion Wins Many a Game

Earlier in this chapter the mating powers of the newly promoted Queen were mentioned. In Diagram 48 we have a position of the greatest practical importance.

Remove White's Pawn and the game is a draw. (A lone Bishop cannot force checkmate.) But with the Pawn

Diagram 48 (*White to play*)

BLACK

WHITE

ahead, White can simply advance it, giving it adequate protection until it reaches the eighth rank. Then White promotes the Pawn to a Queen, and the win is child's play.

One final example (Diagram 49) will show the tremendous dynamic power unleashed by a newly promoted Pawn.

Diagram 49 (*White to play*)

BLACK

WHITE

Black has a Queen for a mere Pawn, and he is actually threatening checkmate by . . . *Queen to King Rook 4 check* (. . . Q–KR4ch) or . . . *Queen to King Rook 8 check* (. . . Q–KR8ch).

But luckily for White, it is *his* turn to move, and he completely changes the course of the game.

He plays *Pawn to King Knight 8 (becoming a Queen) check* — or P–KN8(Q)ch. Black's King must move out of check, allowing White's new Queen to capture Black's Queen. And White wins!

In Diagram 49 White had only a Pawn against a Queen. Nevertheless, the promotional power of White's Pawn proved stronger than Black's already existing Queen!

These examples give you an impressive picture of the power of Pawn promotion. You can now see that the Pawn is much more important than most players realize. You can also see why it is bad policy to be careless about losing Pawns. *Every Pawn is a potential Queen.*

Looking Ahead

In the next three chapters we shall take up the basic opening, middle-game, and endgame ideas essential to winning chess. As you read these chapters, you will want to keep in mind the three strongest moves: checks, captures, and Pawn promotions.

At every point in every game you play, you want to ask

yourself these three routine questions until it becomes second nature to ask them:

Is a check possible?
Is a capture possible?
Is there a passed Pawn that has queening possibilities?

Once you have formed the habit of asking these questions, you have made very substantial progress toward becoming a good player — *a winning player.*

CHAPTER 7

"HOW DO I GET STARTED?"

Five Basic Rules for Opening Play

"I don't know what to do!"

"How do I form a plan?"

"I just make any old move."

"I'm completely bewildered."

Rueful remarks like these more or less sum up the way inexperienced players feel at the start of a game.

Some players are so puzzled that they fly to the opposite extreme. They clamor for a foolproof plan that will provide the whole course of the future play.

No chess book can do the whole job, nor would we want it to. We want our own initiative, our own spontaneity, our own fun in playing our own game.

We cannot expect to be infallible. Even the multimillion-dollar electric brains are not infallible. There is the story of a scientist who had developed a mechanical calculator capable of doing the most complicated problems in jigtime. On one occasion when the machine was being demonstrated, an exceptionally difficult problem was given to the electric brain.

The scientist pushed a button. The machine banged and clattered and hissed. Bright lights flashed on and off as its "innards" heaved to solve the problem. At last, after a loud crash the answer appeared: "Drop dead!" Something had gone wrong.

Some such result bedevils us when we try to follow instructions too literally and too far. So let us try to find some *generally helpful procedures,* instead of looking for infallible methods.

Simple Plans Are Best

The main difficulty of most players at the start of a game, as we've seen, is lack of plan.

To get over that hurdle, you don't need a very elaborate plan of campaign. Many skillful public speakers will tell you they can deliver a much more effective public speech from rough notes of a few *basic* ideas than from a completely prepared talk in which every last syllable is spelled out and every semicolon is carefully indicated.

The same idea applies to chess as well. What you need for the opening stage are a few basic rules that will work because *they apply to all kinds of opening positions.*

And because these rules *do* work, they will keep you out of trouble; they will give you confidence; they will provide the momentum for reaching the middle game with a promising position.

"I had a foolproof plan to win, but you didn't play your pieces the way I expected you to."

Five Basic Rules

These basic rules can be expressed in both positive and negative form. We'll state them both ways, for some people learn best from such instructions as, "Keep off the grass." Others find more meaning in such instructions as, "Stay on the sidewalk."

So here are the five basic rules:

1. Bring out your pieces and Pawns so that they bear on the center squares of the board.
   (*or:* Don't neglect the center squares.)
2. Develop your pieces rapidly.
   (*or:* Don't neglect your development.)
3. Develop your pieces effectively.
   (*or:* Don't make repeated moves with the same Pawn or piece.)
4. Guard your King against enemy attack.
   (*or:* Don't ignore the welfare of your King.)
5. Postpone the development of the Queen.
   (*or:* Don't play out the Queen early in the game.)

Control the Center

By "the center" we mean the central group of squares indicated by crosses in Diagram 50.

We know from a vast amount of experience that pieces

Diagram 50 (*White to play*)

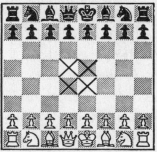

BLACK

WHITE

are placed at their best *in or near the center*. From this sector they can move rapidly to any other part of the board.

On the other hand, a piece that is kept at home is ineffectual. And if played to the side of the board, a piece is generally out of the battle.

If you place Pawns in the center, you prevent hostile

Diagram 51 (*Black to play*)

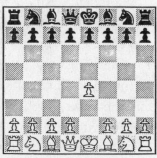

BLACK

WHITE

pieces from moving to the squares commanded by those Pawns. For that reason *Pawn to King 4* (P–K4) is a splendid opening move.

Your first move has accomplished a number of important things for you. It places the King Pawn on an important center square. It prevents your opponent from bringing any of his pieces to Queen 5 and King Bishop 5, *the two squares commanded by your Pawn at K4.*

Nor is this all that this first move accomplishes for you. Study Diagram 51 and you will observe that the King Pawn's move has opened the diagonal of your King Bishop (now still at home). You have also made it possible for your Queen to move. However, you do not want to move that piece too early in the game.

Now what should Black do? On this point he can consult the great Tchigorin, one of the outstanding masters of the nineteenth century.

When Tchigorin had White, he played *Pawn to King 4* on his first move and felt that he had the better of it. When he had Black, he answered his opponent's *Pawn to King 4* by playing . . . *Pawn to King 4* in the sincere conviction that he had at least an even game.

This may sound like bad logic, but it is good psychology, and we shall adopt it. Black answers . . . *Pawn to King 4* (. . . P–K4) and thus gives his position all the benefits White obtained from the same move.

Let's sum up the first rule in this way, then: *Play to control the center, and always play out the King Pawn on your first move.*

(If you're playing Black, answer *Pawn to King 4* with
. . . *Pawn to King 4*. If White starts with *Pawn to Queen
4*, you reply . . . *Pawn to Queen 4*.)

Diagram 52 (*White to play*)

BLACK

WHITE

Develop Quickly

To win games, you have to put your pieces to work.
They exert no force while roosting on their initial squares.

To "develop" pieces means to play them out so they can
come to grips with the enemy. The faster you develop, the
faster you can become aggressive.

Now back to Diagram 52. You can play out your King
Knight or you can develop your King Bishop. What should
your choice be?

Well, let's see. Bishops move on diagonals and they
sometimes have a choice of several possible squares on a

diagonal. Thus, you can play *Bishop to Queen Bishop 4* (B–QB4); although *Bishop to Queen Knight 5* (B–QN5) may seem desirable a little later.

Suppose, on the other hand, we consider moving out the King Knight first. Can we reach an immediate decision about where to move the Knight? Yes, we can.

We have a choice of *Knight to King Rook 3* (N–KR3); or *Knight to King 2* (N–K2); or *Knight to King Bishop 3* (N–KB3).

Diagram 53 (*Black to play*)

BLACK

WHITE

This is the position we will have if we play *Knight to King Rook 3* (N–KR3). It is not inviting, for the Knight has little scope at King Rook 3. It has only three possible moves, none of them to a square located in the center. (Because of its short hopping move, the Knight is best placed in the center.)

For these reasons, we rule out *Knight to King Rook 3* (N–KR3). And precisely for these reasons, Knights are very rarely played to squares on the Rook files. Now let's consider another possibility: *Knight to King 2* (N–K2).

Diagram 54 (*Black to play*)

BLACK

WHITE

This is the position we reach after *Knight to King 2* (N–K2). This development is also not inviting, although the Knight does have five possible moves from the King 2 square.

Another merit of playing the Knight to King 2 is that it strikes at the Queen 4 square—one of the vital center squares.

But these advantages are completely canceled out by the fact that the Knight at King 2 *blocks the development of White's King Bishop.*

Always distrust opening moves that block the development of some other piece!

Now only one other move is left for White's King Knight. That move is shown in Diagram 55: *Knight to King Bishop 3* (N–KB3).

Diagram 55 (*Black to play*)

BLACK

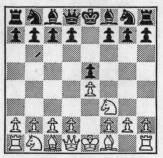

WHITE

Diagram 55 shows the position we reach after *Knight to King Bishop 3* (N–KB3).

The more we study this move the more it appeals to us. First, the Knight *attacks* Black's King Pawn and threatens to capture it. *Development plus attack* is the most economical form of development there is. Black is already on the defensive.

Secondly, on King Bishop 3 the Knight has far more scope than the Knight gets from playing to King Rook 3 or King 2.

Note also that the Knight strikes at *two important center squares* — King 5 and Queen 4. This tells us the Knight has a fine future at King Bishop 3.

A final point — at this square the Knight does not block the development of White's King Bishop.

Now we come to two conclusions:

1. *The King Knight should almost invariably go to King*

Bishop 3 in the opening. *You can forget about the alterna-*
tive possibilities for this Knight.

2. We know where we want to develop the King
Knight, whereas the King Bishop's development is still in
doubt. *Therefore we develop the King Knight before the*
King Bishop.

Let's return to Diagram 55, to see how Black proceeds.
He needs to protect his King Pawn, and he ought to do it
with a developing move. The answer, as seen in Diagram
56: . . . *Knight to Queen Bishop 3* (. . . N–QB3).

Diagram 56 (*White to play*)

BLACK

WHITE

Black has done well. His King Pawn is defended.

Now it is White's turn, and the logical move is to play
out his Bishop. He has two moves, either one quite good:
Bishop to Queen Bishop 4 (B–QB4), or *Bishop to Queen*
Knight 5 (B–QN5).

This is an example of simple, purposeful development

that will serve you well in game after game. Thus your opening problems are greatly simplified.

You can pay a heavy price for neglecting your development; therefore, don't lose valuable time by running after some decoy Pawn. Such a chase will cost you time and effort. It will leave you way behind in development and very likely expose you to sharp retaliation.

Don't make one Pawn move after another — as many players do because they don't understand the value of development. Take the following position, after each side has made six moves:

Diagram 57 (*White to play*)

BLACK

WHITE

White has played out both his center Pawns; he has developed both Knights to their best squares; he has developed his King Bishop; he has castled, bringing his King into safety.

In short, White has achieved a great deal in six moves. What has Black done? He has moved six Pawns, and his utterly miserable position offers no promise whatever. Broadly speaking, many games are won or lost in the opening. Here it is no exaggeration to say that Black has lost the game in the opening.

Develop Effectively

This rule tells us it is not enough to develop rapidly; we must also develop *effectively*. In other words, bring pieces out to their best squares — *the squares on which they do their best work.*

In Diagrams 53 and 54 we see poor development of White's King Knight. In Diagram 55 we see splendid development of this same Knight.

Again in Diagram 56 we see that Black played out his Queen Knight with maximum effect. This piece is now admirably developed.

Suppose we take another look at Diagram 56. White wants to play out his King Bishop. But where should this piece play? Suppose White tries *Bishop to Queen 3* (B–Q3).

The development of the Bishop to Queen 3 is development, to be sure — but very bad development.

Why is this so?

The Bishop move is shortsighted because it blocks White's Queen Pawn and *therefore makes it impossible to develop White's other Bishop.*

Diagram 58 (*Black to play*)

BLACK

WHITE

This second Bishop cannot move until the Queen Pawn advances and makes room for the development of the Bishop.

On the other hand, suppose White plays *Bishop to Queen Bishop 4* (B–QB4), producing the following position:

Diagram 59 (*Black to play*)

BLACK

WHITE

This Bishop development is excellent. The Bishop bears down effectively on the important center square Queen 5 and points menacingly along the diagonal leading to the neighborhood of the Black King.

At the same time White's Queen Pawn is free to advance, so that the development of White's other Bishop is not held back.

Now for the negative aspect of this rule: Don't make repeated moves with the same piece or Pawn.

When a player has no opening plan and no opening rules to go by, he is very likely to move the same piece — or Pawn — repeatedly.

The result is that he falls far behind in development, with a loss of time that is generally impossible to make up. You can avoid these repetitious moves by moving a piece to its best square and leaving it on that square.

Protect Your King

The initial position of your King, on a center file, is not a good one. As more and more pieces swing into action, you will find the King is exposed to heavy attack.

Therefore you do well to castle early and tuck away your King at the side of the board where it will be hard for the enemy to strike at the King.

Let's see how this is accomplished from the position of Diagram 59. Black plays . . . *Bishop to Queen Bishop 4*

(. . . B–QB4) and in reply White castles. This leads to the following position:

Diagram 60 (*Black to play*)

BLACK

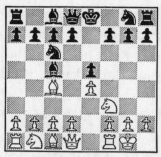

WHITE

Now White's King is much safer than it was at its original square. Meanwhile White has brought his King Rook to a square where it plays a more active role than at its original corner square.

Getting your King into safety by castling is one of the most important moves in the game. But if you look back a bit, you see that White's castling was made possible by his playing out his King Pawn, his Knight, and his Bishop.

So there you see an additional and automatic value of development: it helps you castle early and assure the safety of your King.

Of course the same reasoning applies to Black in Diagram 60. His immediate task is to play . . . *Knight to King Bishop* 3 (. . . N–KB3). He will then be ready to castle and get his King into safety.

Avoid Premature Queen Moves

Playing out the Queen early has a great fascination for many players, because they are awed by the great power of this piece.

However, it is precisely the power of the Queen that makes it vulnerable. Take the situation in Diagram 61, where White has aimlessly played out his Queen at a very early stage, attacking three Pawns that are all defended.

Diagram 61 *(Black to play)*

BLACK

WHITE

White's last move was *Queen to Rook 5 (Q–R5)*. Black's reaction to the meaningless Queen move is a disdainful "So what?" He plays . . . *Knight to King Bishop 3 (. . . N–KB3)*, developing with gain of time.

The Black Knight thus plays to its best square. At the same time it attacks White's wayward Queen, which must waste a move for abashed retreat. Then it is Black's turn to move again. White has lost the initiative.

Early Queen moves must at least have the justification of working in combination with another piece. When the Queen goes gallivanting in the early stages of a game, it is fairly certain that it will return home with nothing accomplished.

Summary

What have we learned about opening play that can help us to be winners at chess?

Here are the main points for playing the opening effectively:

1. Try to concentrate your forces in the center. Always start the game by moving the King Pawn or Queen Pawn two squares.

2. Develop your pieces quickly. Always play your King Knight to King Bishop 3.

3. Develop pieces effectively — to their best squares. Beware of making too many Pawn moves — or too many moves with the same piece or Pawn.

4. Be sure to castle early to protect your King against enemy attack. Developing your pieces promptly clears the back row for early castling.

5. Avoid playing out the Queen for Pawn-grabbing expeditions. These only lose time and expose your Queen to threats of capture.

These rules are easy to follow. Often you will find that following one rule enables you to follow another one at the same time. For example, if you will develop your pieces consistently, you will avoid useless Pawn moves.

Above all, following these rules helps you to be a winner at chess because they give you an objective; they give you a method for starting the game. This spots you a definite advantage over the vast majority of players who start the game in a mood of aimless drifting.

Aimlessness is a likely prelude to losing. Purposeful play is an aid to setting up winning positions.

CHAPTER 8

"WHAT DO I DO NOW?"

Two Basic Rules for the Middle Game

Once upon a time a tenderfoot found himself mounted on a very spirited horse. During its antics, the animal got one of its hoofs stuck in a stirrup.

The queasy rider happened to look down and noticed what had happened. In mingled alarm and relief he shouted, "If you're getting on, I'm getting off!"

That expresses the mood of the player who, after handling the opening fairly well, suddenly finds himself confronted with the complexities of the middle game.

This is indeed an important problem, because the middle game is the very essence of chess. This is the stage where the pieces are out, ready for action, the Queens have unleashed their full power. The battle is on, and . . . well, what do we do about it?

To begin with, you already possess some powerful weapons for winning in the middle game; you know the importance of scrutinizing every position for possible checks or captures.

The middle game is especially rich in complicated situations. These are the positions that abound in violent possibilities, such as checks and captures.

And precisely because middle-game positions are so complex, they are the ones in which oversights are most likely. If you're on the alert for checks and captures, you'll avoid such slips and pounce on your opponents' oversights.

Aside from this important feature, there are two simple rules that will often guide you to victory in the middle game. These are:

Give your pieces mobility.
Make your pieces co-operate.

Wilhelm Steinitz, who was World Champion, for almost three decades, knew the secret of handling the pieces with the greatest economy — the secret of getting the most out of each piece.

Once he was asked how it was possible for him to give the odds of a whole Rook, that is, start the game with one of his Rooks removed. "It's easier than you think," he replied in substance. "I do this only against weaker players. I understand just what each piece can accomplish, while these weaker players are all at sea.

"Since they don't make the best use of their pieces, they are really the ones that are giving the odds — not I! In the middle game, all my pieces are forcefully in play. Their pieces are mostly at home. Naturally I have the best of the bargain."

The player who does not use his pieces to best advantage is simply helping his opponent to win the game.

Give Your Pieces Mobility

You've seen that pieces must be developed not only *quickly* but *effectively*.

Effective development means that the pieces have mobility, elbowroom. If your Rooks are on long, open files; if your Bishops strike along long diagonals, they cover a lot of ground and menace the opponent's forces.

On the other hand, if your pieces are blocked by obstacles; if your Bishops are hemmed in by your own Pawns; if your Knights are off to the side, then you're headed for trouble. *If your pieces lack mobility, then your opponent has the initiative.*

Diagram 62 is a good example of superior mobility:

Diagram 62 (*Black to play*)

BLACK

WHITE

Black is definitely the attacker. How can we tell?

Black's Rooks are doubled on the half-open Queen Bishop file. Two Rooks placed on the same line exert tremendous pressure if it is open or if they have an enemy target.

In this case the Rooks attack the weak white Pawn on the Queen Bishop file. Note this: *Black attacks the Pawn, White defends it. Black's Rooks have a great deal of mobility, White's Rooks have very little.*

What about the Queens? Black's Queen is well advanced, and attacks White's Queen Rook Pawn. The White Queen has very little scope, and is busy defending the Queen Bishop Pawn and the Queen Rook Pawn. This is menial work for a Queen.

Again we see the same picture: Black's Queen attacks, White's Queen defends.

What about the Knights? Both Knights bear on the center, so apparently there is not much to choose here. Actually there is a very important distinction to be made:

If White plays *Knight to King 5* (N–K5), he attacks nothing. If Black plays . . . *Knight to King 5* (. . . N–K5), he attacks the White Queen and the weak White Queen Bishop Pawn.

Thus the search for capturing threats yields the right move for Black: . . . *Knight to King 5* (. . . N–K5). (See Diagram 63.)

What is Black's threat? He attacks White's Queen. This threat is made possible by the excellent mobility of Black's Knight. It occupies one of the center squares on which a Knight is most effective.

Naturally White can move his Queen away from attack. But more than that is involved.

Diagram 63 (*White to play*)

BLACK

WHITE

In Diagram 62 White's Queen Bishop Pawn was attacked twice and defended twice, and is therefore safe from capture. But in Diagram 63, while the same Pawn is still defended twice, it is attacked *three* times. Consequently, after White moves his Queen away he loses his Queen Bishop Pawn.

Superior mobility enabled Black to win material.

In the next position (Diagram 64), White has no immediate gain of material in view. Still, his lead in mobility is very striking.

White's development has been *fast*. How can we tell? He has four pieces developed, whereas Black has only two pieces out. (A rough-and-ready count will always be a good check in comparing the amount of development on both sides.)

White's development has also been *effective*. Both his Bishops strike along impressive diagonals. His Knight is splendidly posted in the center ("centralized").

Diagram 64 (*White to play*)

BLACK

WHITE

This last point is very important. As you've seen in connection with Diagrams 53 and 55, it makes a very big difference whether a Knight is marooned at the side of the board, or whether he is posted in the center, the busy crossroads of the chessboard.

One last important feature: so far there is only one completely open file, the Queen file. (We say a file is "open" when there are no Pawns on it.)

Now White can bring a Rook to the Queen file and then play *Rook to Queen* 2 (R–Q2). After that he will bring his other Rook to the Queen file — "doubling" the Rooks on the Queen file. Thus White will get a hammer-lock control of another important open line.

Can Black dispute this control of the open file? Certainly not in the immediate future. He can bring only one Rook to the open file. His other Rook, still on its home square, is hemmed in by his *undeveloped* Knight and Bishop.

Because Black failed to develop rapidly in the opening,

he now finds that his pieces are still on the back row, while White's are actively in the fight. This is another proof that if you want to be a winning player, you must develop your pieces rapidly.

If anything, Black's position in Diagram 65 is an even more impressive example of superior mobility.

Diagram 65 (*Black to play*)

BLACK

WHITE

Let's break this position down into its elements, as we've done previously.

Black's Rooks are doubled on the half-open King Bishop file. As we've seen, doubling the Rooks on a single line gives them great power.

Note that the King Bishop file isn't open at all as far as White is concerned. His Rook on that file is blocked by his own Pawn.

Now to further comparisons: note the magnificent sweep of the long diagonal commanded by Black's Bishop. Posted on a remote corner, the Bishop cuts right across the board. White's Bishop, on the other hand, has no scope to speak of.

Compare the White and Black Knights. The White Knight is back on its home square, accomplishing nothing at all. As for the Black Knight, it is superbly centralized on the vital center square, Queen 5. The Knight, which can never be driven away from its outpost, hits out in all directions from its centralized location.

This is definitely a winning position for Black. Superior mobility adds up to winning play.

Make Your Pieces Co-operate

As we've seen several times, *effective* development is just as important as *fast* development.

When you develop your pieces effectively, you can make them co-operate toward achieving a certain objective. If you don't develop effectively, you will find later on that your forces are scattered and cannot be made to work together. Take Diagram 66 as a telling example.

White's pieces are certainly developed, but to no good purpose. His Rooks are disconnected — the one at Queen Knight 7 is in a particularly bad way. It is unprotected, subject to sudden attack, and completely isolated from the other White forces.

The White Knights are off to the side. Realistically speaking, they are out of the game. The White Bishop,

Diagram 66 (*Black to move*)

BLACK

WHITE

blocked by its own Queen Pawn, accomplishes nothing.

Worst of all for White is the fact that his King is exposed to attack, and his far-off forces are no help to the King. Only the White Queen stands by to help, and this piece cannot do all the work.

Black stands to win if he can profit by White's inept, inharmonious set-up. So let's appraise Black's formation.

His Queen is beautifully posted right in the heart of the enemy position. And because White's forces are miserably situated, they cannot drive the Black Queen away.

The Black Queen has the co-operation of the Bishop at King Rook 4 and the well-centralized Knight at Queen 4.

The Black Rooks do not take part in any attack on the White King, but they mutually protect each other, which is more than can be said for the White Rooks.

All Black's advantages, in short, add up to a winning position for him. To hope for any resistance on White's part, we would need the optimism of the little girl who

"Spike can't be disturbed now. He's in the middle game."

asked God "to make the bad people good, and the good people nicer."

Black's winning move is . . . *Knight to King Bishop 5* (. . . N–KB5). Diagram 67 shows the resulting situation:

Diagram 67 (*White to play*)

BLACK

WHITE

As the result of the powerful Knight move, Black has two brutal threats. One is: . . . *Knight to King Rook 6 check* (. . . N–KR6ch). This would fork White's King and Queen and consequently win White's Queen.

The other threat is . . . *Queen takes Rook* (. . . QxR). Black's twofold threat, which cannot be completely parried, exploits the scattering of White's forces.

When your forces co-operate skillfully, they often succeed in concentrating on an enemy target which is both valuable and vulnerable. Diagram 68 is a good example.

White's forces have a great deal of mobility; Black's pieces have very little scope. White's black-square Bishop

Diagram 68 (*White to play*)

BLACK

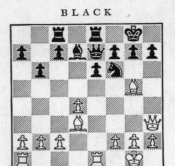

WHITE

pins the Black Knight. The Bishop is *active*, the Knight is *passive*. (If Black moves the Knight, he loses the Queen.)

Black's Bishop is blocked by its own King Pawn. The White Bishop, on the other hand, draws a bead on Black's King Rook Pawn. This is no mere figure of speech, as White's Queen also attacks this weak point.

Of course, in the position of Diagram 68, White cannot play *Queen takes Rook Pawn check* (QxRPch). The Black Knight parries this threat.

Yet White can make this threat real by first playing *Bishop takes Knight* (BxN), removing the protection of Black's King Rook Pawn.

What made White's attack so powerful in this example? It was his superior mobility and the smooth co-operation of his Queen and two Bishops concentrating on a weak point.

Another example of powerful co-operation appears in Diagram 69:

Diagram 69 (*Black to play*)

WHITE

Studying the position of Diagram 69 reminds us that the quickest way to understand any middle-game position is to look for differences.

White's King, for example, is perfectly safe and unapproachable. Not so the Black King, which is back in the center of the board.

No Black pieces menace the White King. In the case of Black's King, a White Rook has penetrated all the way to King Rook 8, and its presence so deep in Black's position is very disturbing to the defender.

Equally alarming for Black is the presence of White's Queen at King Rook 7. The far-advanced White Rook and Queen have the co-operation of still a third White unit, the King Rook Pawn; and here is where danger rears its ugly head.

Why? White is threatening *Pawn to King Rook 6* (P–KR6), *pinning* the unfortunate Black Knight which cannot move; to do so would expose Black's King to attack.

When we look for moves to parry this threat, we realize that the exposed position of his King is not Black's only difficulty; he also suffers cruelly from a lack of co-operation among his forces.

Let's emphasize this again, because there is a moral to this that can be applied to win repeatedly.

White has three units that co-operate powerfully to bring about the downfall of Black's King. The other White units do not co-operate in this project — but neither do they hinder, nor are they afflicted with any weakness that might distract White from his winning maneuver.

Black's pieces, on the other hand, do not work together. They are scattered, jumbled. Their present ineffectual state is the result of thoughtless, creeping development.

Finally Black decides to "unpin" his Knight at King Knight 2. He gets his King off the vulnerable line by playing . . . *King to King 1* (. . . K–K1), leading to Diagram 70:

Diagram 70 (*White to play*)

BLACK

WHITE

Black's despairing King move has not affected the basic ailment from which his position suffers. His position still remains crowded, his pieces are still crippled by bad communication.

White now plays *Pawn to King Rook 6* (P–KR6) and Black discovers to his horror that his unfortunate Knight is still pinned! For if the attacked Knight moves, there follows *Queen takes Rook* (QxR). This is the kind of punishment that overtakes a player when his pieces do not co-operate and consequently become vulnerable to enemy attack.

The two basic techniques, then, for winning in the middle game are to give your pieces as much mobility as you can, and to see that they co-operate with each other. As you try to achieve these objectives, you will also strengthen your opening play. As you develop your pieces in the opening, you will ask yourself, "Will these pieces be active later on?" and "Can they work together, or will they be separated from each other?"

This will lead to an improvement in your play that will help you to win more games. As you give more attention to the middle-game factors, you play the opening more thoughtfully. As your handling of the opening improves, in turn, you achieve more promising middle-game positions. It all adds up to better chess — winning chess.

CHAPTER 9

THE ENDGAME IS THE PAY-OFF

Five Basic Rules for Endgame Play

Some years ago I saw a picture of two chimpanzees "playing" chess. The picture was good for a laugh, but it reminded me of an interesting experiment.

This experiment was devised by scientists who wanted to find out whether chimpanzees could be induced to work. By lifting an eighteen-pound handle on a "work machine," the chimpanzees could obtain a poker chip. When they inserted the chip in a slot machine, they received a grape for their efforts.

The animals took to these machines with astonishing skill, yet one feature was striking: as soon as the chimps were no longer hungry, they stopped work.

It would be impossible to apply the psychology of the chimps to chess. All the moves of a game make up a single unit. In chess, we can't quit when we're ahead. Unlike the indolent chimps, we have to play out the game to a finish. And that is what makes the endgame so important.

In a game of chess the endgame is the pay-off. This is

the concluding stage, reached when most of the pieces have been traded off. Here a player pushes his advantage to a logical conclusion — if he can. If he has gained material, he uses his extra material to enforce checkmate or to queen a Pawn — if he knows how.

To "know how" is the secret of good endgame play. Five basic principles stand out when it comes to playing the endgame effectively. Here they are:

1. Know the elementary checkmates.
2. Have your King play an active role.
3. Utilize passed Pawns.
4. Post Rooks on the seventh rank.
5. Simplify when you have a material advantage.

Know the Elementary Checkmates

When you are ahead in material and your opponent refuses to resign, you may be called on to force checkmate. This makes it essential for you to know the elementary positions in which you can checkmate with minimum force.

The checkmate of King and Queen against King is the easiest. Diagram 71 shows a standard mating position.

Another standard mating position with King and Queen against King is shown in Diagram 4 in Chapter 1.

When we come to checkmating with a Rook, we are confronted with a somewhat harder problem. The Rook

Diagram 71 (*Final position*)

BLACK

WHITE

can force checkmate only in the manner of Diagram 4, not in the manner of Diagram 71.

Whether checkmating with Queen or Rook, it is necessary to drive the enemy King to one of the sides of the board. Diagram 72 shows a typical Rook mating position:

Diagram 72 (*Final position*)

BLACK

WHITE

One Bishop cannot enforce checkmate, but two Bishops

can. The two-Bishop mate requires forcing the enemy King into a corner. Diagram 12 (page 43) shows the final mating position with two Bishops.

The checkmate with Bishop and Knight also requires "cornering" the enemy King. This checkmate is shown in the following diagram:

Diagram 73 (*Final position*)

BLACK

WHITE

In all these elementary checkmates, it is clear that the King of the winning side makes an important contribution to the setting up of the checkmate position. This leads to the second basic principle.

Have Your King Play an Active Role

To avoid any confusion about this advice, remember that it applies *only to the endgame.*

In the opening and middle game, the chief role played by the King is that of a target. In these earlier portions of the game, with all or most of the pieces on the board, the King is best handled by being kept away from the scenes of greatest activity.

But in the endgame most of the pieces have disappeared. The danger to the King is greatly reduced. At last the King can venture forth and play an active part in the game.

To say that the King should be active means that this piece should be *centralized*. Once in the center, the King is ready to move fairly quickly to any sector of the board. Diagram 74 illustrates this point effectively.

Diagram 74 (*Black to play*)

BLACK

WHITE

Here both Kings are centralized, but Black's Pawns are vulnerable, and White's King is more aggressively placed.

Suppose, for example, Black plays . . . *King to Queen 3* (. . . K–Q3). White replies *King to King Bishop 5* (K–KB5), winning a Pawn on the next move.

This will give White a passed Pawn, which he can then advance until it reaches the eighth rank and becomes a Queen.

Or, coming back to Diagram 74, suppose Black plays . . . *King to King Bishop 3* (. . . K–KB3). In that case White plays *King to Queen 5*, again winning a Pawn and winning the game in the same way.

In Diagram 75 Black's King is effectively centralized:

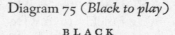

Diagram 75 (*Black to play*)

Black plays . . . *King to King Bishop 6* (. . . K–KB6). This aggressive move carries a threat of a subsequent move of . . . *King to King 7* (. . . K–K7), forcing White's protective Knight to move — after which Black can capture White's King Bishop Pawn with an easy win.

(Note in all these examples that the advancing King is in no danger because the material has been reduced considerably.)

Diagram 76 offers another example of a powerfully centralized King:

Diagram 76 (*Black to play*)

BLACK

WHITE

Black's King is so far advanced that White is practically paralyzed.

Black wins here by advancing the Pawns on the Queenside, where he has four Pawns to three.

First he plays . . . *Pawn to Queen Knight 4* (. . . P–QN4) and . . . *Pawn to Queen Rook 4* (. . . P–QR4) and . . . *Pawn to Queen Knight 5* (. . . P–QN5). Then, after several Pawn exchanges, Black reaches the position of Diagram 77.

Black now plays . . . *Pawn to Queen Bishop 6* (. . . P–QB6) forcing a passed Pawn that will win quickly for him.

These examples reveal the vast power unleashed by the King in the endgame stage. Skillful maneuvering with the

"I refuse to resign. You'll have to fire me."

Diagram 77 (*Black to play*)

BLACK

WHITE

King will win many an endgame in which the material is even at the start.

Utilize Passed Pawns

In Chapter 6 you saw many examples of the promotional powers of the Pawn. Most endgames center around the struggle to turn a passed Pawn into a Queen.

Inexperienced players are unaware of the strength of a passed Pawn, and thus miss many winning opportunities. Diagram 78 shows how quickly a passed Pawn can lead to victory.

White's Knight is attacked. Instead of bothering to defend this piece, White plays an astounding move: *Pawn to King 6* (P–K6). The passed Pawn advances!

After Black's reply . . . *Bishop takes Knight* (. . .

Diagram 78 (*White to play*)

BxN) White has still another remarkable move: *Pawn to King 7* (P–K7). This leads to the following position:

Diagram 79 (*Black to play*)

If Black captures the White Rook, White advances his King Pawn to the eighth rank, obtaining a new Queen.

And so, in the position of Diagram 79, Black has nothing better than . . . *Rook to Queen Bishop 1* (. . . R–

QB1). When the Pawn advances to the eighth rank, becoming a Queen, Black's Rook captures the new Queen.

White recaptures with his Rook. He thus remains with Rook against Bishop — an easy win for White.

Diagram 80 offers another convincing example of the power of a passed Pawn:

Diagram 80 (*White to play*)

BLACK

WHITE

In this position, with material even, most players might find no feature worthy of special notice.

Actually there is a factor here which gives White an easy victory. His Queen Rook Pawn is a "remote passed Pawn" — a weapon against which Black is helpless.

White plays *Pawn to Queen Rook 4* (P–QR4). If Black makes no effort to stop this Pawn, it will go right on to the queening square. Consequently, Black must play . . . *King to Queen 1* (. . . K–Q1) in order to capture the sinister passed Pawn.

But now Black has abandoned his Pawns to the inroad

of the White King. White answers *King takes Pawn* (KxP), and proceeds to capture the remaining Black Pawns as well, after which he will be in a position to queen one of his remaining Pawns.

These examples indicate how you can make use of passed Pawns to win in the endgame.

Post Rooks on the Seventh Rank

Still another characteristic and formidable endgame weapon is the placement of a Rook on the seventh rank.

When you post a Rook on the seventh rank, you are generally attacking several hostile Pawns. The need for defending them ties down your opponent's forces and gives you a strong initiative. It often happens in the course of the endgame that you can advance your King to add to the pressure.

Diagram 81 is a good example of the possibilities resulting from seventh-rank penetration.

One big distinction which we noted in several middlegame positions also appears here.

White's all-powerful Rook is *active*, Black's purely defensive Rook is *passive*. Similarly, Black's King is burdened with the job of guarding his King Knight Pawn; whereas White's King is poised for activity.

Note the enormous scope of White's Rook. To the right, it attacks Black's King Knight Pawn and ties Black's King

Diagram 81 (*White to play*)

BLACK

WHITE

to the defense of this Pawn. To the left, White's Rook attacks the Queen Rook Pawn and ties Black's Rook to the defense of this Pawn.

Thus strict passivity is Black's role in this ending. White, on the other hand, has two winning possibilities: one is to bring his King to King Knight 6. This will win Black's King Knight Pawn, followed by the win of more Pawns.

White's other winning method is to bring his King to Queen Rook 6. This will win Black's Queen Rook Pawn, followed by the win of more Pawns.

From this characteristic diagram you can realize the stifling pressure exerted by a Rook on the seventh rank — in the heart of the enemy position. This maneuver will often assure you victory in the endgame stage.

The principle of the seventh rank can be extended still further: Rooks are always most effective in aggressive setups. Passivity is often fatal.

Simplify When You Have a Material Advantage

Frank Marshall, the leading American master for many years, once gave this sage advice: When you have the better of it, play simply. When the game is going against you, look for complications.

There is an important moral here for the player who has obtained a material advantage. Simplicity is in his favor. Why? Because if the game proceeds along tranquil lines, he will go on to turn his material advantage into victory.

On the other hand, complicated play often leads to confusion or inconsistency or lack of concentration on the main goal.

Here is the recommended course:

When you are ahead in material, seek Exchanges that will make it easier for you to use your material advantage while at the same time avoiding needless complications.

Diagram 82 (*White to play*)

BLACK

WHITE

This usually involves getting rid of the Queens. As the Queen is the strongest piece, removing the Queens is the surest way to rule out complications.

Diagram 82 shows one way of simplifying.

White, who is a Pawn to the good, wants to simplify the position by exchanging Queens. He achieves his purpose by playing *Queen to King 4 check* (Q–K4ch). This forces the Exchange of Queens no matter what Black does. Once the Queens are off, White has a straightforward ending, with no middle-game problems to be considered.

What will his winning plan be? He has four Pawns to three on the Queen-side. He will advance these until, by means of Exchanges, he obtains a passed Pawn. He will then aim to queen the passed Pawn. These tasks become a lot easier with the Queens out of the way.

A different technique solves the same problem in Diagram 83:

Diagram 83 (*White to play*)

BLACK

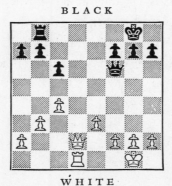

WHITE

White has two ways of forcing the immediate Exchange of Queens. Let's consider one way: *Queen to Queen 4* (Q–Q4).

This move offers the Exchange of Queens and also threatens *Queen takes Queen Rook Pawn* (QxQRP).

Black is already a Pawn down. If he evades the Exchange of Queens, he will lose a second Pawn — a loss that he cannot afford. He therefore plays . . . *Queen takes Queen* (. . . QxQ) and White replies *Rook takes Queen*. Again the complications have been removed.

This example ends our study of the five basic principles of endgame play. You will find that knowing and applying these principles is very rewarding, for few players are familiar with endgame technique. Playing the endgame well will be an immense help to you if you want to become a winner at chess.

Here, once again, are the five important principles of endgame play:

1. Know the elementary checkmates.
2. Have your King play an active role.
3. Utilize passed Pawns.
4. Post Rooks on the seventh rank.
5. Simplify when you have a material advantage.

"YOU CAN'T MOVE THAT PIECE!"

Winning by Pinning

In chess, they say, the threat is stronger than its fulfillment. A threat which hangs over a player's head like the proverbial sword of Damocles may cause him great uneasiness. On the other hand, the execution of the threat brings at least the relief of getting rid of the suspense.

Among chess players, the mental anguish caused by threats may take strange forms. Take the case of a famous grand master named Nimzovich who hated smoking in all its forms. If an opponent tried to smoke during a tournament game, Nimzovich headed like an arrow for the tournament director and protested bitterly.

One day Nimzovich was paired to play Vidmar, another outstanding master. Vidmar was a great cigar smoker, but he abstained in deference to Nimzovich's well-known hatred for smoking.

However, Vidmar could not resist teasing Nimzovich by setting out his cigar case on the chess table. Nimzovich eyed the cigars nervously for hours. Finally he could no longer restrain himself and rushed off with his complaint to the tournament director. After listening patiently to Nimzovich, the official was baffled.

"But you admit he hasn't smoked, so what are you complaining about?"

"True," Nimzovich replied, wringing his hands; "but he THREATENS to smoke, and you know with us chess players the threat is stronger than the fulfillment!"

The Irritating Pin

Of all the different kinds of threats, the pin is undoubtedly among the most irritating.

The pin is an attack by a Queen, a Rook, or a Bishop on an enemy unit that screens another unit from attack. In Diagram 85 (page 153), for example, Black's Bishop at Queen Bishop 4 is pinning White's Knight. The Knight in turn screens White's King from attack.

A pin of this kind, where the King is the screened piece, is called an "absolute" pin. The pinned piece cannot move, because that would expose the King to attack. This is prohibited by the rules of chess.

Sometimes a piece may continue to be pinned for a long time. In some cases it may be attacked several additional times, for in chess it's praiseworthy to hit a chessman when he's down. Even where the pressure is not increased, it is very burdensome to be subject to a nagging pin. Many a

"He hopes to win by pinning."

time a long-standing pin has goaded a player into some impatient dash for freedom that quickly proved fatal.

The pin, then, is a powerful weapon in several ways. To be familiar with it is of great practical value, for pins are probably the most frequent kind of attack seen on the chessboard. A good working knowledge of pins will win many games for you.

How Pins Work

The quickest way to appreciate pins and learn how to use them is to study some devastating examples. Diagram 84, for example, shows the tremendous power of the absolute pin.

Diagram 84 (*White to play*)

BLACK

WHITE

Black's King and Queen stand on the same diagonal.

Note that this is a white-squared diagonal, and that White has a Bishop traveling on the white squares.

Do these three features mean something to you? Perhaps not. Then note another factor: White can play *Bishop to King Bishop 5* (B–KB5). The Bishop is guarded by the White Rook at King Bishop 1.

The Bishop move sets up a pin! Black cannot save the Queen because moving the Queen away would expose the Black King to attack — and that is strictly forbidden.

So, no matter how Black plays, he loses his Queen for only a Bishop. White's gain of material gives him a winning advantage.

In Diagram 85 the pin is already in existence.

Diagram 85 (*Black to play*)

BLACK

WHITE

Black pins the White Knight, which cannot move lest it expose the White King to attack.

Black attacks the Knight, White defends it with his Rook. Black's problem is this: can he strengthen his attack

on the helpless pinned piece? Indeed he can. By playing
. . . *Pawn to King 4* (. . . P–K4) Black wins a whole
piece.

The pinned Knight, attacked by a mere Pawn, cannot
retreat and must go lost. Again the pin has led to a winning
material advantage.

Such examples by no means exhaust the winning possibilities of pinning moves. Diagram 86 offers a refined
example of what the pin can accomplish.

Diagram 86 (*White to play*)

BLACK

WHITE

Of course White can pin the Black Queen by playing
Rook to Queen 4 (R–Q4). As in the position of Diagram
84, this move would win Black's Queen — if only White's
Rook were *protected!* It seems that we must regretfully
give up the pin.

Must we forget about the pin — or do we have a hidden
resource? Suppose White tries *Rook to Queen 4* (R–Q4)
and Black replies . . . *Queen takes Rook* (. . . QxR).

Now comes White's sly surprise — a check! He plays *Pawn to King 6 check* (P–K6ch), leading to the position of Diagram 87.

Diagram 87 (*Black to play*)

BLACK

WHITE

Black is lost!

The deadly check has incidentally opened up a line of attack by the White Queen against the Black Queen. Black must take care of the check. In so doing he is helpless against White's coming *Queen takes Queen* (QxQ). This capture leaves White with a winning material advantage of Queen vs. Rook.

There you have a splendid example of how pins are invented if they don't already exist. Here's another fascinating example which if anything is even more tricky (see Diagram 88).

White is a piece down; he has given up a piece to arrive at this position. Just why did he do that?

True, White can regain the piece by exchanging

Diagram 88 (*White to play*)

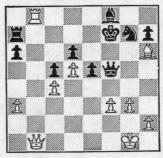

Queens and then playing *Rook takes Bishop check*
(RxBch). But this listless line certainly offers no hope
of winning. Whatever White has in mind must be a lot
more forceful than this.

We want something forceful and we want a pin. *The
most forceful move of all is a check,* so the answer is: *Rook
takes Bishop check* (RxBch). Black has no choice: he must

Diagram 89 (*White to play*)

answer . . . *King takes Rook* (. . . KxR). This gives us the position of Diagram 89.

White is now a Rook down. Ordinarily this would be a hopeless material disadvantage, but White knows what he is doing. He has produced the pin he was looking for: Black's Knight is pinned!

White plays *Queen takes Queen check* (QxQch) and Black cannot recapture! So White has the winning material advantage of Queen vs. Rook.

Double Play

When you can combine the pin with a fork, then your opponent is headed for real trouble.

A fork (as shown in Diagram 34, page 75) is a double attack, generally carried out by a Knight. This type of attack is difficult to parry at the best of times. But when the two types of attack are combined in one nasty threat, the pressure is generally irresistible.

Diagram 90, for example, is a prelude to havoc.

Black's King and Queen are pitiably vulnerable to a fork. Or at least they would be if Black's King Pawn did not protect him against *Knight to King Bishop 5 check* (N–KB5ch).

But is the work of the King Pawn really effective, or is its protection only a fake? After all, the Pawn is pinned by White's Rook at King 1.

Diagram 90 (*White to play*)

BLACK

WHITE

Therefore White's winning move is *Knight to King Bishop 5 check* (N–KB5ch). If Black captures the Knight, then he loses by *Rook takes Queen* (RxQ). If Black does not capture the Knight, then he loses by *Knight takes Queen* (NxQ). Either way, Black's loss of material is fatal.

In Diagram 91 the pin and the fork are combined with a blunderbuss effect.

Diagram 91 (*White to play*)

BLACK

WHITE

White has two pins here: his Bishop at Queen Rook 3 pins Black's Rook at King 2. Secondly, Black's King Bishop Pawn is pinned on the open King Bishop file.

White takes advantage of the double pin by giving the forking check *Knight to King 6 check* (N–K6ch). Diagram 92 pictures the resulting extraordinary situation:

Diagram 92 (*Black to play*)

BLACK

WHITE

The checking Knight cannot be captured by the Black Rook, which is helpless because it is pinned.

Neither can the checking Knight be captured by Black's King Bishop Pawn, which is also pinned.

And so Black is condemned to look on helplessly and let his Queen be captured by the galloping Knight.

From these examples you can gain a convincing idea of the strong, persistent pressure that pins exert. Once you start making use of pins, you will find endless opportunities to win games with them. Pinning chess is winning chess.

CHAPTER 11

"GIVE TILL IT HURTS!"

Winning by Sacrificing

Perhaps you have heard what happened when St. Peter and St. Paul came down from heaven to play a round of golf. After both saints had shot several amazing holes-in-one, St. Peter was fed up. "That's enough," he muttered; "let's cut out the miracles and play golf."

Chess isn't like that at all. Miracles are an ordinary, everyday occurrence in chess. What could be more miraculous than winning games by deliberately losing material?

How Sacrifices Win

This notion is paradoxical and puzzling. Again and again you have seen emphasized the idea that you must avoid losing material. Sacrificing material — offering it or allowing it to be captured — seems to be without rhyme or reason.

Still, we're told that sacrificing material can win games. There can be only one way to explain this riddle:

The only way to justify intentionally losing material is that *you expect to gain something of greater value than the value of the material sacrificed.*

There is the idea that clears up the mystery: *the gain of greater value.* For example, to give up your Queen is a cheap price to pay for an immediate checkmate. To give up your Knight is certainly no blunder if in return you win your opponent's Queen.

Let's try a very simple example, as shown in Diagram 93:

Diagram 93 (*White to play*)

BLACK

WHITE

When we're told that White plays *Knight to King Knight 6 check* (N–KN6ch) in this position, we wonder whether he's out of his mind. After all, the Knight can be captured in two different ways.

But have you noticed this — that in the act of giving

check White uncovers a discovered attack by the White Queen against the Black Queen? Black must of course pay heed to the *check*.

The result is that after Black has cleared the offending Knight out of the way, White plays *Queen takes Queen* (QxQ) with a crushing advantage in material. The sacrifice has proved profitable.

In Diagram 94 the sacrificing is much more subtle and much more expensive. But in due time it leads to checkmate, justifying all of White's strenuous efforts.

Diagram 94 (*White to play*)

BLACK

WHITE

There are two key factors in this situation: Black's forces are scattered and do not co-operate. Worse yet, as far as Black is concerned, his Queen is out of play.

Yet at the moment White does not seem to be making headway, for his Queen is attacked and the Pawn fork . . . *Pawn to Queen Bishop 5* (. . . P–QB5) is threatened.

Summing up the plus and minus features, we see that time is of the essence. How can White press home the attack?

White starts with a sacrifice: *Knight to King Bishop 5 check* (N–KB5ch).

Black must capture the obstreperous Knight with his King Knight Pawn. But now a line of attack has been opened up against Black's King.

White immediately seizes this line with *Rook to King Knight 3 check* (R–KN3ch). Note that White is operating with checks — forcing moves par excellence. His Queen is still attacked, but Black must get out of check.

Black plays . . . *King to King Bishop 1* (. . . K–KB1). Now White can simply capture the Bishop and win, but he has another fine sacrifice.

Now White's most forceful move is *Rook to King Knight 8 check* (R–KN8ch). It takes imagination to find

Diagram 95 (*Black to play*)

BLACK

WHITE

"Of course, I remember what day it is. It was nine years ago today I checkmated Reinfeld in 12 moves."

such a move, which looks absurd on the face of it. But it is a *check* and therefore forces Black's hand. Diagram 95 shows the resulting situation.

Black plays . . . *King takes Rook* (. . . KxR), which is of course forced.

But now White has a checkmate in three moves. He plays *Queen to King 8 check* (Q–K8ch), leaving Black one reply: . . . *King to King Knight 2* (. . . K–KN2).

White's next move is *Queen takes King Bishop Pawn check* (QxKBPch), and now it is mate next move.

Thus, if Black plays . . . *King to King Rook 3* (. . . K–KR3), White answers *Queen takes Bishop mate* (QxB mate).

And if Black tries . . . *King to King Rook 1* (. . . K–KR1) instead, White mates by *Queen to King Knight 8 check* (Q–KN8ch) or even *Queen to King Bishop 8 check* (Q–KB8ch).

All this is beautifully played and calculated, but what makes it possible? The scattered position of Black's forces, and the Black Queen's leave of absence.

Sacrificing the Queen

The two previous examples show how it is possible to give up substantial material in the right kind of situation and still win the game.

But now we come to a really sensational theme — sacrificing the Queen. It seems unbelievable that a player can part with this most powerful of all chess pieces and still win the game.

This is playing for high stakes and the occasion is nothing less than forcing checkmate. In all such cases, there has to be some overriding reason that makes the sacrifice feasible.

In Diagram 96 the sacrifice is feasible because Black's King is not properly protected. In fact, the timely escape of the King is blocked by Black's own pieces.

Diagram 96 (*White to play*)

BLACK

WHITE

White's first move comes as a shock: *Queen takes King Rook Pawn check* (QxKRPch). Black must take: . . . *King takes Queen* (. . . KxQ).

Here, too, White operates exclusively with checks. After giving up the most powerful piece on the board, he has to rely on the most forcing type of move — the *check*.

White's next is *Rook to King Rook 5 check* (R–KR5ch).

This forces . . . *King to King Knight 2* (. . . K–KN2). Note that Black's King is strictly on its own; it gets no help from the other Black pieces, which now stand by helplessly.

Now comes another check: *Bishop to King Rook 6 check* (B–KR6ch), leading to the position of Diagram 97:

Diagram 97 (*Black to play*)

Black plays . . . *King to King Rook 2* (. . . K–KR2). The retreat with the King to King Rook 1 would lead to the same finish.

Now White plays *Bishop to King Bishop 8 discovered check* (B–KB8 dis ch) and Black is checkmated! A very beautiful line of play!

Again we must emphasize that the Queen sacrifice paid off because Black's pieces did not co-operate and because Black's King was not protected.

In Diagram 98 there is again a logical basis for a Queen sacrifice.

Diagram 98 (*White to play*)

BLACK

WHITE

Black's King is in the center and White is very considerably ahead in development. Again Black's forces do not co-operate and the Black King will have to fend for himself. Only by this type of analysis can we perceive that the miracle of the Queen sacrifice has a reasonable and logical basis.

What actually inspires White's Queen sacrifice is the realization that Black's Bishop at Queen Bishop 3 has the chore of stopping a very nasty discovered check against the Black King. But this Black Bishop also has the job of protecting the Black Knight. This gives White the winning idea:

He plays *Queen takes Knight* (QxN). If Black is not to remain a piece down, he must play . . . *Bishop takes Queen* (. . . BxQ).

But now that Black's Bishop has left the Queen Bishop 3 square, White has a devastating double check. The only way for White to find compensation for his sacrificed

Queen is in peremptory checks that leave Black no avenue of escape.

White proceeds with a check — a double check, in fact. His next move is *Knight to Queen Bishop 7 double check* (N–QB7 dbl ch), leading to the position of Diagram 99:

Diagram 99 (*Black to play*)

BLACK

WHITE

You may recall from the discussion of Diagram 23 (page 57) that you can't interpose a piece to a double check. There is only one reply, and that is to move your King.

And so Black has only one move: . . . *King to King 2* (. . . K–K2).

White now continues *Rook to Queen 7 check* (R–Q7ch) and Black is checkmated! A very beautiful line of play.

And in Diagram 100, too, Black has a sound reason for his miraculous Queen sacrifice.

In this case it is the White King that is vulnerable in the

Diagram 100 (*Black to play*)

BLACK

WHITE

center of the board. And once again we find magnificently co-operating pieces fighting against scattered forces.

Black begins with the startling capture . . . *Queen takes Bishop check* (. . . QxBch).

White replies *King takes Queen* (KxQ). As in the previous examples, the sacrifice of the Queen must be followed up by forthright checks. And so Black continues with . . . *Bishop to King Rook 3 check* (. . . B–KR3ch).

The check forces White's reply: *King to King Bishop 5* (K–KB5). From move to move the White King has become more exposed. A glance at Diagram 101 reveals the critical state of the White King.

In this curious position Black can force checkmate by giving a discovered check with his Knight. ANY move of his Knight discovers check and gives checkmate!

With these examples we conclude our study of how to

Diagram 101 (*Black to play*)

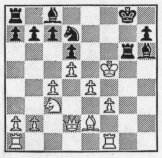

WHITE

be a winner at chess. Sacrificing material — losing it *for a purpose* — is the hardest but most enjoyable form of winning chess.

In reading this book you have seen what it takes to be a winner at chess. Checkmate is always our goal, but we need to know the most effective ways of reaching that goal.

We need to concentrate on the three strongest kinds of moves — checks, captures, and Pawn promotions. In regarding the game as a whole, we want to develop our pieces rapidly and effectively. We want to put them to good use in the middle game. And in the endgame we want to reap the fruits of our previous good play.

The lesson of the last two chapters is that there are two winning techniques we can use in any part of the game. One of these is the pinning attack, the most frequent and one of the most effective of all types of attack. The other technique is that of sacrificing material in order to win back even more than was sacrificed.

These are the ways to become a winner at chess. May this book help you to get more victories out of your chess — and more fun, too!

A REFRESHER:

The Basic Rules of Chess

Most readers of this book are familiar with the basic rules for playing chess. For the benefit of those who do not know the rules or may have forgotten some of them, here is a summary of the essentials.

A game of chess is played on a board made up of 64 squares in eight vertical and eight horizontal rows.

Each player has sixteen chessmen. The player of the light-colored pieces is called "White." The player of the dark-colored pieces is called "Black."

Here is the opening position (see Diagram 102):

Each side has eight Pawns — these are in the second and seventh rows ("ranks").

Each side has two Rooks — these are in the corners.

Each side has two Knights — these are next to the Rooks.

Each side has two Bishops — these are next to the Knights, proceeding toward the center of the board.

Now we have left the King and Queen.

The King has a small cross in his crown.

The Queen is to the immediate left of the King in Diagram 102, the opening position of a game of chess.

Note that the White Queen is on a white square. The Black Queen is on a black square.

White always moves first.

Diagram 102

BLACK

WHITE

How the Pieces Move

The King can be moved to a square adjoining the square he occupies.

The King can never move to a square which is under attack by a hostile piece. The reason for this will be explained a little later on.

In Diagram 103 the King can move to any square next to the one on which he is now placed. This gives him a choice of 8 moves.

The Queen can move vertically, horizontally, or diagonally — in eight different directions. The Queen's move along one of these lines is limited only by occupation by other pieces of some square along a given line.

Diagram 103

BLACK

WHITE

In Diagram 104, believe it or not, the Queen has 27 possible moves!

The Queen has 3 possible captures and 24 other moves. No other piece on the chessboard remotely approaches such power. This enormous cruising range helps to explain why the Queen is the most powerful of all the pieces on the chessboard.

Diagram 104

BLACK

WHITE

The Rook can move horizontally (along a rank) or vertically (along a file). It moves along any one of several lines until it reaches an already occupied square. In Diagram 105 the Rook has a choice of 14 possible moves. These moves include the capture of the Queen or Knight.

Diagram 105

BLACK

WHITE

The Bishop moves only on diagonals — rows of squares of the same color. One Bishop moves only on white squares, the other on black squares.

In Diagram 106 the Bishop has a choice of 13 moves.

The Knight has an L-shaped move of three squares. It can be described as one square to the left or right and then two squares straight up or down. Another way of describing it is one square straight up or down and then two squares to the left or right.

In Diagram 107 the Knight has 8 possible moves.

A peculiarity of the Knight is that it is the only one of

Diagram 106

BLACK

WHITE

the chess pieces that can hop over its own or enemy men. This is not the same as capturing; the pieces it hops over stay put.

The Knight can capture only on the squares to which it can move. In Diagram 107 the White Knight can capture the Black Knight or Pawn.

Diagram 107

BLACK

WHITE

How the Pawn Moves

The Pawn is the weakest of the chessmen, but it has many interesting features.

One important point is that it can move *forward* only.

It moves one square at a time. However, any Pawn that is still on its original square has the option of advancing one square or two.

In Diagram 108, the Pawn on the right can advance one square or two. The Pawn on the left can advance only one square.

Diagram 108

BLACK

WHITE

Diagram 108 suggests still another point about Pawn moves. White Pawns in diagrams move up the page. Black Pawns in diagrams move down the page. Each diagram in this book is labeled "Black" at the top and "White" at the bottom to remind you of the direction *from* which a Pawn is moving.

How the Pieces Capture

The chess pieces — the King, the Queen, the Rook, the Bishop, and the Knight — all capture the same way they move.

In Diagram 103 the White King can capture the Black Pawn.

In Diagram 104 the White Queen can capture the Black Rook or the Black Knight or the Black Bishop.

In Diagram 105 the White Rook can capture the Black Knight or the Black Queen.

In Diagram 106 the White Bishop can capture the Black Rook or the Black Bishop.

In Diagram 107 the White Knight can capture the Black Pawn or the Black Knight. (If it is Black's turn to move, his Knight can capture White's Knight.)

More about the Pawn

The capturing powers of the Pawn have been left to a special section because *it is the only one of the chessmen which does not capture the same way it moves.*

The Pawn captures one square ahead to the right or left.

Thus in Diagram 109, the White Pawn can capture the Black Queen or the Black Knight. The White Pawn cannot capture the Black Pawn.

Diagram 109

One of the unusual features of Pawn play is that Pawns can capture *en passant*, or in passing. Diagram 110 shows a typical instance of this. If the Black Pawn advances one square, White's Pawn can capture it. So far, so good.

But if the Black Pawn advances *two squares*, the White

Diagram 110   Diagram 111

Pawn can capture it in passing. *The White Pawn is then on the sixth rank, just as if the Black Pawn had advanced one square and had then been captured.*

Diagram 111 shows the position reached after Black's Pawn advances two squares and White captures it in passing.

Still another feature of Pawn play deserves attention. If a Pawn marches all the way down to the eighth rank without getting captured, you can promote it to a Queen or a Rook or a Knight or a Bishop. For the importance of this, see pages 81–96.

More about the King

The object of a game of chess is to bring about a position where the hostile King is attacked and cannot escape from attack. This is known as "checkmate," and it explains why the King can never move to a square which is under attack by a hostile piece. Diagram 4 on page 20 is an example of checkmate.

An attack on the King, whether fatal or not, is called a "check." Diagram 1 on page 17 is an example of a check.

To assure the King's safety, the King is empowered to "castle" with one of his Rooks. "King-side castling" and "Queen-side castling" are illustrated in Diagrams 112 and 113. The first diagram shows the position before castling; the second show the position after castling.

Diagram 112   Diagram 113

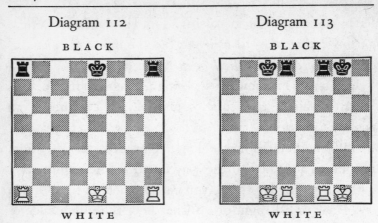

To castle on the King side, you play your King two squares toward the nearer Rook and then place the Rook on the other side of the King.

To castle on the Queen side, you move your King two squares toward the farther Rook and then place the Rook on the other side of the King.

Note that you can't castle in reply to a check (though you may castle later on). If you move your King, you forfeit the castling privilege altogether.

Games may end in a draw by mutual agreement, or by perpetual check, or by lack of checkmating material (page 93), or by stalemate. This last refers to a position where the King is not in check and is forced to move into check. Diagram 114 is a case in point.

Diagram 114 (*Black to move*)

BLACK

WHITE

How to Record Moves

In order to be able to record moves, we have to give each square on the board a name.

This is how we do it: each of the pieces in the opening position (Diagram 102) has a specific name. The Bishop next to the King is called the King Bishop. The nearby Knight is the King Knight, and the Rook next to the Knight is called the King Rook.

The pieces next to the Queen are the Queen Bishop, Queen Knight, Queen Rook.

The horizontal row on which these pieces stand is called the *first* rank. Consequently, the square the King Bishop stands on is called King Bishop 1. The square the Queen stands on is Queen 1, etc.

Each Pawn is named for the piece in back of it. Thus the Pawn in front of the King is called the King Pawn and stands at King 2. If it moves ahead two squares, we write the move "Pawn to King 4."

The vertical rows on the board are called "files." They are named for the pieces that stand on them at the beginning of the game. The file the King Rook stands on is the King Rook file. The first square is King Rook 1; the second square is King Rook 2, and so on, all the way down to King Rook 8.

All these details are easy to grasp; but here is a point that troubles many players. White records his moves from his side of the board, while Black records *his* moves from *his* side of the board.

Thus, the square that White calls King 4 is King 5 from Black's side of the board. White's Queen 2 square is Black's Queen 7 square. (Note that these numbers always add up to 9.)

However, if you remember that you must reckon the names of the squares from the side that is making the move, you will have no trouble whatever with the chess notation.

INDEX